A Long Journey to the
White Picket Fence & Green Grass

Estella Victoria Frederick Shivers

Butku's Corn Island Publications
The Villages, Florida

ISBN-13: 978-1547246311 / ISBN-10: 1547246316

Butku's Corn Island Publications
2351 Baton Place
The Villages, FL 32162

Cover and Logo Photo by Kai-Yvonne Shivers
Cover Design by Mary Lois Sanders

Dedication

This book is dedicated to my husband John
and to my children—Eric, Lashonne, and Kai-Yvonne,
for they have attentively listened to my story as they offered their
valuable suggestions.

A special dedication is to my siblings—
Tomas Orlando, Glenda, and Eleanor,
for they also have endured tremendous hardships
during their childhood years as I did.

Figure 1: Estella V. Frederick at 22

Acknowledgements

I give thanks to my children for listening to my stories. Their questions brought back memories I had never talked about. I also thank my sisters Glenda and Eleanor for sharing their thoughts that contributed to my story.

I thank Donald Marchand for his assistance in my getting started and his wife Rena for her patience, which allowed him the time to do so.

I give thanks to the Creative Writers Group of The Villages, Florida, for their well-intentioned critiques and help when presenting my story. Their questions and suggestions have allowed me to polish where needed, thereby giving a full explanation of various occurrences.

I especially thank Mary Lois Sanders for her guidance, intelligence, and patience in my writing this story. I could not have written it without her! I am forever grateful.

Table of Contents

Table of Photographs

Introduction

I, Estella Victoria Frederick Shivers, the fourth and last child of Hetrudes and Lyn Hurst Frederick, was born on June 17, 1944 in Bluefields, Nicaragua, Central America. On the night I was born, I have been told, my father walked the floors with me in his arms as he whispered sweet words in my ears. Six months later he left for a job on a ship that traveled around the world.

Unknown to me, father left in pursuit of a better way of life that would allow him to provide for us, his family. He took the advice of his male family members and applied for a position on a passenger boat, which accepted him to fill the position as a Bos'an's Mate. Unfortunately, I would not meet up with him again until I reached the age of nine.

This story tells of the hardships our family endured while he was away, as well as his commitment to us that led me to where I am today.

In my heart, I forgive him for the years we were left behind, and I thank him for coming to our rescue when he brought us, his children, to America. The rest is up to us to follow in his footsteps, for he has taught and served us well. May God Bless and Keep our Papa!

Chapter 1—Birth of the Fourth Child

I expect that most of the people reading this would have been born in a hospital under a doctor's care, but the majority of children in suburban areas of Nicaragua were not so fortunate. Most of the births were delivered by midwives in the home.

My family lived in the small city of Bluefields, Nicaragua. We were a family of six. Within this household lived our father Lyn Hurst, our mother Hetrudes, along with my eight-year-old brother Tomas Orlando, seven-year-old sister Glenda, five-year-old sister Eleanor, and me.

We lived in a small house; however, our home was large enough to hold our family in a comfortable manner. It was built of wood and placed on top of three-foot high wooden posts raising it from the ground (some houses sat on large rocks, as you'll see in the next photo). Placing them above ground was to prevent Nicaragua's dangerous snakes from entering, as well as to provide protection from flooding. The roof was made of tin, which served as a crashing harmonic orchestra when it rained hard, or a lullaby when it rained softly, the different sized raindrops tap, tap, tapping different sounds that sang us to sleep.

Most houses were built with an attached porch where families gathered to simply chat while their children told their made-up stories before turning in for the night. Neighbors often stopped for a minute or two simply to exchange friendly words as they passed by, for the folks in this small village were very familiar with each other's lives.

We were a melting pot of Spanish, Black, White, East Indian, and Chinese in which people were identified as "Creole"—a combination of these nationalities.

The churches in our neighborhood were Anglican (Episcopal), Moravian, and Catholic.

Figure 2: My mother Hertrudes & the House Built on a Rock Foundation

It was my father's choice that his family join the Anglican Church. We were baptized, attended Sunday morning worship, and religious school. The churches also provided education to those willing to attend.

The students who went to public school or religious school were taught in Spanish, and were assigned to wear the country's designated uniform— girls wore white blouses, blue ties, pleated blue skirts, blue socks, and black shoes; boys wore white shirts, blue ties, blue pants, blue socks, and black shoes.

In Bluefields there were three grocery stores. We also supplied ourselves by raising chickens, pigs, cows, and by fishing. The foods we grew were cassava, plantains (large bananas for cooking only), potatoes, breadfruit, bananas, and coconuts. At times, we treated ourselves by buying cooked food from the Chinese store.

The languages we spoke were English and Spanish; however, people coming from another country would speak their own language amongst themselves.

At this time, we managed to live quite comfortably. When our father was away because of his employment as a seaman, he made sure to send money to our mother to support us. However, as time went by, payments to our mother lessened and life changed for the worse.

Figure 3: Map of Nicaragua

Note: Bluefields was the name given after a Dutch pirate Henry Blufeldt, who had hidden in the bays during the 17th century. Its population is about 60,000 consisting of Mestizo, Miskito, Creole and Garifuna, Chinese, Smu, and Ramas. Nicaragua borders Honduras to the North and Costa Rica to the South. Note: You can see the Corn Islands off the coast in the Caribbean Sea.

Chapter 2 — My Birth, As My Mother Told Me

And so it was, that my mama was walking from town after shopping with my six-year-old sister Glenda. Glenda was carefree and barefoot walking along an unpaved and dusty road. It was hot, but gentle ocean breezes helped cool them down as they walked and talked. Little Glenda was a chatterbox, and just seemed to enjoy talking about nothing in particular. Mama always seemed to enjoy these little chats.

Mama was nine-months pregnant, and after walking quite a distance back home she suddenly felt a sharp cramp. Having had three children already, this labor pain was no secret unexpected thing. She stopped and sat on a tree trunk, feeling that she couldn't go any further.

"Glenda, run home as fast as you can and get Papa to come here, for I need help."

Glenda, in a state of panic, ran as fast as her little legs could take her, calling for Papa as she ran. Finally seeing him, she tried to tell him what was happening but was so animated that gibberish was all that was coming out of her mouth.

"Calm down, child, just tell me slowly, everything will be fine."

"Mama is in pain and needs you to come and help her. Please Papa, hurry, she's sitting on a tree trunk on the road from town," Glenda explained.

"I'll go get Mama, and I want you to go and get the midwife and bring her here," said Papa.

Glenda ran off, praying that Miss Victoria would be home, and my father ran to get Mama and quickly carry her home.

Miss Victoria, the local midwife, was a large woman with a perpetual smile. Like local doctors who carried their medical bags with them, she had her own that she kept filled with lots of white towels, a silver pan to heat water, and other instruments of her trade. She wore a white dress, which distinguished her immediately as a midwife.

Entering our home, Miss Victoria shouted, "I'm here, Mr. Frederick, ready to help."

"Thank you for coming so quickly, Miss Victoria. I'm so glad that you were available. Come into the bedroom."

She entered the bedroom to begin her examination of Mama, and was not surprised that the baby was coming very quickly. She went through her normal preparations, readying the towels, heating the water, and sat down in the family rocking chair. As any experienced midwife did … she just sat and waited for the blessed event.

On or about 12:30 a.m. I was born, and as with most fathers who see their newborn child, it was declared by Papa that I was "the most beautiful baby he had ever seen!" I suspect he had said that about all my sisters and my brother when they were born, and he always whispered it to me whenever he had a chance.

Papa and Mama had already decided to name me Estella, and then Papa said to Miss Victoria, "You've always been there when we needed you and so we have decided that Estella's middle name will be Victoria in your honor."

And that is how my life began as Estella Victoria Frederick.

Chapter 3—Mother's Difficult Decision

My father was employed as Bos'an's Mate on the passenger ship the SS Constitution that traveled around the world. Unfortunately, these voyages would last an indefinite amount of time—some six months or more.

Because our father was gone, the chore of raising four children, which now included me, a newborn infant, became much too difficult for mother to handle. She decided to leave Bluefields and live with her mother on Big Corn Island. My grandmother would lend support in raising us, and she and Mother would also provide companionship for each other.

Big Corn Island is approximately forty-five miles from the mainland and can be reached by boat, ferry, or airplane.

Figure 4: Big Corn Island

Aerial view of Big Corn Island, which has a paved road about 12 kilometers (7.5 mi) long running the length of the island. The Corn Islands are about 70 kilometers (43 mi) away from Bluefields. Corn Island Airport in the city of Brig Bay is served by La Costeña airlines from Bluefields and Managua. Big Corn Island can be reached by a ferry that departs once a day from El Rama through the Río Escondido with its mouth at Bluefields. The port is at Southwest Bay on Big Corn Island (World Port Index No. 9775). Little Corn Island is accessible by a ferry that departs from Big Corn Island.[1]

****

Before going to the island, the funds mother received from our father were no longer enough to cover expenses. Miss Maggie Valley, a close friend of the family, became aware of mother's struggle, and offered that our family move in to live at her home until we were ready to relocate. Mother accepted this offer while making plans to live with her mother.

Early one morning we approached the house of Miss Maggie, where she sat in her usual position in her rocking chair on the veranda. She quickly stood up to welcome us, as she revealed the most comforting smile. "Hetrudes, come right in. Please make yourself and your children comfortable. You can stay here as long as you need." We stayed for a while prior to our move.

Mother responded with a sad, "Thank you, Maggie. I hope to leave for Corn Island by next month. Thank you so much."

When Papa learned of mother's decision to relocate, he returned briefly to lend his assistance. He also learned of mother's hardship with the behavior of their nine-year-old son Orlando, so they decided to send him to live with his grandfather at the Grand Cayman Island, British West Indies. There he would be raised by his grandfather.

Papa also believed it was best that his son be raised by a man and not by a woman. With this in mind, it was only natural that he alone explained to his son that this was his intention.

Once this decision was made, mother sobbed and sobbed, but there was nothing left for her to do. So, Papa sat with little Orlando and told him of his plans.

"Orlando, I'm sending you to live with your grandfather

---

[1] Wikipedia.com

Swan at the Grand Cayman Island. Your mother tells me you are always staying out of school and misbehaving. It seems that you need a man to handle you, so that is where I'm sending you. Now do remember that I love you very much and this is the best thing for me to do."

"But Papa, I don't know anyone there." Orlando looked at his father with sadness.

"Your grandfather will take good care of you. You will get to meet all your uncles, aunts and cousins who live there, so don't be afraid. I'll also check on you from time to time."

"O.K., Papa, I'll behave. But I'll miss you and Mama," Orlando responded with tears in his eyes.

"I know you will son, but I promise that one day we will all be together again." Papa looked at Orlando with a promise and a sad smile.

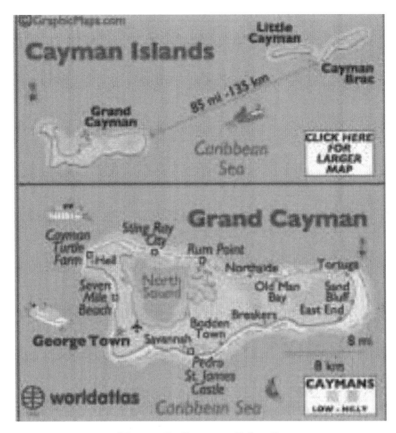

Figure 5: Cayman Islands

Note: The Grand Cayman Island is the country of my father's birth, where he was the first born of fifteen children, so there were enough brothers and sisters remaining at home to assist in raising his son. Unfortunately, since this island is a far distance from Nicaragua, Mother would not see her son again for 20 years.

Figure 6: Cayman Islands in The Caribbean

The **Cayman Islands** are a British dependency and island country. It is a three-island archipelago in the Caribbean Sea, consisting of Grand Cayman, Cayman Brac, and Little Cayman. Georgetown, the capital of the Cayman Islands is 438 km (272 mi) south of Havana, Cuba, and 504 km (313 mi) northwest of Kingston, Jamaica. The islands lie between Cuba and Central America. Georgetown's geographic coordinates are 19.300° north, 81.383° west.[2]

---

[2] Wikipedia.com

Chapter 4—Father's Departure from His Family as Told by Papa

One month had passed since our father had come home for a visit, and now it was time to return to work. Unfortunately, his employment as a *Bos'an's* Mate on a passenger ship would keep him away for several months at a time. For this reason, he held his newborn baby with admiration; for he knew it would be a long time before she would be in his arms again.

He walked the floor with Baby Estella, as he whispered in her ears, with words only intended for her to hear. "Estella, you're such a beautiful baby, I don't want to put you down."

Father admired his baby girl continuously, while revealing a special father's love and admiration.

When overhearing these words of my father, Mother turned to him saying with softness in her voice, "Don't worry, Darling. Although I'll live in Corn Island, we'll wait for you to join us there. Just hurry and come back to us."

Early the next morning he was gone.

Chapter 5—Where Is My Father?

I was just an infant when our father departed and his absence didn't affect me. It's obvious a baby can't miss what she's never had. However, as I grew older, I did wonder why I didn't have a father and where he could have gone. I noticed other children with their fathers. Later, all my questions were answered.

My father was hired to work for the SS Constitution and traveled around the world. Since New York City, USA was his home port he decided to move to Brooklyn, New York, where he stayed for many years after. It was convenient, since it was a short distance from the dock.

The SS Constitution was a large and beautiful black and white (Mediterranean) ship owned by the American Export Lines. It was known for its attraction to the rich and famous including several movie stars, including Grace Kelly who sailed aboard the ship on her way to her wedding with Prince Rainier of Monaco. The ship also appeared in several movies ("An Affair to Remember" with Deborah Kerr and Cary Grant, as well as several episodes of the T.V. show "I Love Lucy". Its capacity was over 1000 passengers.

Later I learned that working on a passenger's ship was a demanding job. However, it created the opportunity for merchant marines to work double and triple shifts, allowing them to increase their salary to care for their families in a comfortable manner. It was also a way for them to experience traveling around the world.

Family members often introduced each other to this type of employment, which was the reason my father, his uncles, and son, gained interest in becoming merchant marines. Some family members also worked on oil tankers that made deliveries around the world. To work on such tankers is a dangerous job, for it requires careful handling of these shipments to avoid causing a fire. Also, there were several occasions of overloads, which was said to be the reason for the sinking that caused the life of my father's brother. Unfortunately, his body was never recovered.

Twenty-one years later Father resigned from this prestigious organization. It would be the last of his employment with various shipping agencies, which began when he was only seventeen. At that time, he had to upgrade his age to eighteen. Doing so, allowed him acceptance for employment by a multitude of shipping agencies. Moreover, his outstanding workmanship meant he remained employed with this company for many years.

During the last few years of employment Father's hard work moved him up the corporate ladder. His responsibility was to walk around an assigned area wearing white gloves to swipe where dust was gathered. He would then assign his workers to follow-up with such necessary cleaning.

Unfortunately, the position as merchant marine was the cause that ended many marriages, since husbands were away from their wives for far too many weeks, months and years. My parents were no exception to this rule, for we learned in later years that our father became involved with an American lady and this was the cause that ended the marriage between our parents.

Figure 7: SS Constitution Trans-Atlantic Run to Italy from NYC

Figure 8: SS Constitution - Hawaiian Island Cruising

Figure 9: Manning the Rails

Figure 10: Lyn Hurst Frederick (on the right), Boatswain (pronounced *Bos'an*)

Chapter 6—Life in Bluefields: The Place of My Birth as Told by My Big Sister Glenda

Bluefields is an island where English and Spanish languages are spoken fluently, and the main language is determined according to the town in which we lived. At this time, we resided in an English-speaking town, so English was our main language. There was a Chinatown holding a small population of Chinese immigrants, some of whom owned their own businesses and were capable of communicating with English and Spanish customers.

The streets were often empty of traffic until the school bell rang. Suddenly, after hearing the school bell, an influx of children dressed in uniforms would appear holding their slates beneath their arms on their way to school.

Once school was over children played in the streets; some developed their own games. A famous game was called "Stick-Up". This requires cutting a wooden stick into a sharp point that is thrown into the soft ground (sticking upward) in hopes of knocking the opponent's stick over and on to the ground, i.e., Opponent A throws down their stick into the ground standing it upward (stick-up). Opponent B does the same, in hopes of knocking down their opponent's stick.

This continues until one knocks down the other. If Opponent A's stick is knocked down by Opponent B, it is hit far away by Opponent B (Opponent B uses their own stick to hit it away). Opponent A must fetch their stick and return quickly to throw it down into the ground one time (sticking upward) before Opponent B places their stick into the ground three times, otherwise Opponent A loses the game.

Other popular games were marbles, baseball, and steering bicycle rims. Although the marbles were mostly chipped, their beautiful blue, green, red, and purple colors were very much appreciated by the winner.

Baseball games were very popular and conducted often. Such old dirty baseballs show their wear and tear from previous games, but bounced well enough to bat by a much-used baseball bat.

Lastly, a famous game was to run bicycle rims down the hills controlled with a twisted wire in hand. The wires were formed into a "V" shape to hold both sides of the rim for guidance and better control. It was a mystery to witness the speedy maneuvered bicycle rims, and how the children had the ability to avoid collisions while they raced down the hills. These games were geared toward the boys, but girls were sometimes included.

Playing in the streets of Bluefields was fun until a man with a long white beard appeared out of nowhere. While in the middle of the games a voice from the crowd would call out "Monte-Zuma is coming." Notorious Monte-Zuma was a gentleman who caused the children to run into their houses, for his appearance was dirty and he walked funny. The children were extremely afraid of him, for they considered him to be a frightful sight. He somehow became popular, even though we did not know who he was or where he came from. Once he disappeared, the children returned to the streets to resume their games.

My sister Glenda told me of the day, when I was 1 ½ years old, my dress caught on fire. She was on the veranda when she heard the neighborhood boys shouting to one another.

"Ramon, do you want to play with fireworks?"

"Sure. My big brother gave me a bunch."

"O.K., Ramon, but be careful because the wind is blowing hard."

Shortly after that Ramon's voice rang out, "Tony, watch out … Oh No! The baby is on fire. What did you do?"

Glenda described how I screamed, and screamed, for my dress was on fire. She ran to my rescue and just before the flames reached my hair, smothered the fire with dirt from the ground.

Unfortunately, the flames had already burnt my upper arm close to my face. Fortunately, my face was spared from damage and today when I observe this scar in the mirror, I often wonder how much it must have hurt. However, it is also a remembrance of the day my big sister saved my life.

Chapter 7—Glenda's Near-Fatal Illness as Told by My Mother

Mother's plan to leave Bluefields and live with her mother was suddenly delayed, due to my sister's sudden illness. Glenda became extremely ill with pneumonia, typhoid fever, and an intestinal obstruction. Since the age of three, she had also suffered with asthma attacks on various occasions.

At this time, there was need for immediate financial assistance to cover the expense of a doctor. Most people unable to afford a doctor did not survive such dreadful illnesses. Although father no longer lived with us, mother successfully reached out to him for immediate help and he succeeded in getting money to us. I have often wondered how she knew how to reach him, but I never inquired. Perhaps there was a return address attached to his previous correspondence.

Mother was overjoyed that she could afford a doctor, and with joy in her voice, said, "Glenda, we must be ready when the doctor comes. Your father sent the money, and we have an appointment for today at noon."

"All right, Mama.

Glenda stood up and immediately fell back onto the bed.

"Mama, I need help. I'm too weak to walk."

"Yes, Darling, I know it's hard for you to walk. But Mother is here. I asked Miss Maggie to have the doctor come here and she will have the green bananas ready, so I can feed you when he leaves. You must build up your strength."

"O.K., Mama." Glenda responded in her very faint voice.

"Mama, I lost so much of my hair. Will it grow back?" Glenda was concerned and ashamed about losing her hair due to her illness.

"Oh, Glenda, it's all right. It is more important that you get well and that you're feeling better. Your hair will grow back. You are still beautiful, my Darling,"

We continued living in Bluefields a while longer until Glenda regained her strength, before moving to grandmother's house.

In addition to medical treatment, each day an old island remedy was prepared for Glenda's dinner. This island remedy was to eat a half green banana the first month of her illness, followed by one whole green banana the second month, and one and a half green bananas the third month; all of which were carefully mashed.

Green bananas are not used only for curing the ills, but it is also served with regular meals, and for making soup. Another island specialty is to cook green bananas covered with steamed fish. Although it was believed that green bananas are healthy and is the remedy for many cures, it was difficult to say whether the doctor's treatment or the old island remedy was the one that cured Glenda's illness. However, she was cured!

Chapter 8—Moving in with Grandma Ti-Ti, as Told by My Sister Glenda

Figure 11: L - R - Glenda, our mother Hertrudes, Estella Victoria, Eleanor

A year had passed since my sister Glenda overcame her illness so Mother was now at ease to leave Bluefields to live with her mother. Glenda and I were the only two of her four children to join her in this arrangement, in hopes that our father and other siblings would join us as soon as possible. My five-year-old sister Eleanor was to remain with a lady friend of the family, in order to continue her education at a school governed by a Moravian Church. Our brother Orlando would remain with his grandfather indefinitely.

Since two of Mother's four children were no longer in her possession, she would now have only the two remaining to care for. Although this burden was lifted, she developed a deep sadness compounded by the absence of her husband. However, her plans were to move forward and pray that her family would one day be together again.

Figure 12: Bluefields, Nicaragua - Moravian Mission (far right) & the Sunday School Hall

"Glenda, go and tell your sister Eleanor goodbye and take your baby sister with you. Make sure Estella says goodbye, too. I already said my goodbyes.

"O.K., Mama." Glenda went outside holding my hand to find Eleanor, who was playing with friends.

"Eleanor, we're leaving now. Mama says goodbye."

"Goodbye, have fun." Eleanor turned away, kicking up dust with her shoes as she walked away, with her head bent down hiding her tears.

Glenda sadly turned away with tears in her eyes.

"O.K., Mama, we're ready." Glenda returned to mother holding a small bag ready to leave for the boat.

"Now, let's go into the kitchen to say goodbye to Miss Maggie."

As we entered the kitchen Miss Maggie was busy cooking. She turned to our mother and insisted that we eat before leaving. She instructed that there would be enough time to catch a boat to Corn Island for it was still early morning, about 9:00 a.m., and such travels were scheduled to leave during the afternoon at 12:00 noon.

"Thank you for everything, Maggie. We will eat then move quickly to catch the next banana boat to Corn Island. If my husband comes, just tell him where we are. He knows about my intention to leave Bluefields, but he may stop here first. Tell him that I love him and to hurry and meet us on Corn Island. I want to thank you again for everything. We must be on our way now."

"O.K., Hettie. Take good care of yourself and those children."

"I will. I already said goodbye to Eleanor." Mother turned away slowly with sadness as though she wished she didn't have to leave.

It would take approximately 1½ hours to reach Corn Island from Bluefields, since these two islands are about 45 miles apart by boat. Being familiar with the frequent travels of banana boats, mother knew this would be her best chance of catching a less costly ride. However, it would take additional time, since the boat would make its usual stopover at another island along the way, known as the Bluff.

We arrived at the dock one hour prior to the time of departure. As we boarded a banana boat a tall man stood in front ready to collect our fare. "I see you have two children, Miss. That will cost you $21 cordovans." Mother paid the fare and we walked to a spacious area where we stood, each holding onto a post that reached from the floor to the ceiling. There are no seats in these banana boats for they are simply made of layers to stock bunches of bananas.

We arrived safely to the docks of Corn Island later that Tuesday evening, before dark, and I met Grandmother Ti-Ti for the first time. She had received the message of our expected time of arrival.

I stared at this lady who looked nothing like my mother. She was tall with very dark skin, having tight curly hair that was mixed with grey and black, and she appeared to be of West Indian descent. Ti-Ti was extremely happy to receive us.

Figure 13: Hertrudes (L) & Grandmother Ti-Ti (R)

"Hello Mama, I'm so happy to see you." Mother approached her mother with the happiness that she needed, in order to overcome the sadness from earlier that day.

"Hello, Hettie. I'm so glad you're here. Are these your

beautiful children?"

"Yes. I'll tell you about the other two later."

"But where are they and how could you leave them behind?"

"I didn't want to but that is how things worked out. I'll tell you about it later. Right now, I'm too sad to talk about it."

"O.K., Darling, we'll talk later."

Not waiting for an introduction, Glenda quickly introduced herself.

"Hello, Ti-Ti, I'm glad to meet you. And this is my little sister Estella." Glenda spoke while she looked upward at this tall lady she had never met before.

"Hello, Dearest. You must be Glenda."

"Yes, that's my name," Glenda confirmed.

"Your mother wrote me about you and about your illness. I'm so glad you're feeling better. You all will live with me. I always wondered when I would meet you. Let's go to the house and I'll show you around and where you all will sleep."

We all followed behind our new grandmother as she led us into the house. Ti-Ti lived alone for her husband was deceased. He was of Irish descent, named Livingston Downs, and I never had the pleasure to meet him. He died before I was born.

Ti-Ti had five children: three boys and two girls, all living in Corn Island. Her children took the appearance of a mixed race, some having grey eyes while others had dark brown eyes; some dark skin, others light-skin; some with straight black hair and others with brown wavy hair.

Ti-Ti lived in a wooden house placed on top of a number of large rocks that held it above ground. This prevented entry of the island's dangerous snakes. Although her house was old with gaps between its floorboards, it was kept extremely clean. She did her own cleaning since she lived alone. Her floors were well brushed by the use of a straw broom, beds well-made and the few items she owned were all kept in place.

There were two bedrooms, each holding one bed. One bedroom was for Ti-Ti alone, the other was to be shared by

Mother, Glenda, and me. Mother would have the bed; we children would sleep on the floor.

The house also had a dining room with one table and one chair. The living room contained two rocking chairs and one straight back chair. The kitchen was detached from the house and had what is known as a fireside for cooking. This fireside gave the appearance of a fireplace and was surrounded by logs. There were rocks and sand at its bottom. On top of these was placed the wood for the fire. A stove-like arrangement was also made for baking. This baking arrangement was created by placing an iron pot over the fire. Inside the pot were the biscuits which would bake inside. A sheet of zinc, which held fire, was placed on top of this pot, thereby creating an oven. All types of baking are done in this manner.

There was an outhouse—toilet—located a distance from the house. It had been built many years before and appeared to be old and shabby. Using this outhouse was a scary situation. I required assistance to sit on the edge of the toilet seat inside this old house. It was a dangerous and scary proposition that required either my mother or sister to accompany me and hold my hands as I sat on the edge of the toilet hole. This was the only way to make certain I would not fall in.

At night, our travel to the outhouse was dangerous for there was a multitude of snakes in the area. I preferred to use a chamber pot to avoid walking in the dark or in the rain. However, Grandmother often used a chamber pot during the day which had to be emptied at night and cleaned by either my mother or sister.

A kerosene lantern was used at night as electricity was nonexistent.

Chapter 9—Assisting Mama at the Clothes Line

We led a difficult life in Corn Island, Nicaragua, CA, for our family was extremely poor. Mother did not have the proper education to land her into a higher status of life, but she was successful in keeping food on our plates and clothes on our backs. In order to support us, she washed and ironed clothes for neighborhood families that were able to afford others to do this job. Her customers were aware of the pride she had in her work, which led them to hire her on a regular basis.

Early one morning I heard the sound of splashing waters just outside my bedroom. The window was always open, so I often awakened with the birds and chickens as they created the sounds of an orchestra in its own form. However, the splashing water sounded louder than all of nature's melodies.

I reached across the floor where my sister slept beside me to shake her from her sleep. "Glenda. Did you hear water splashing against the house? Is it raining?" I asked.

She turned her back to me not ready for a conversation so early in the morning, but responded in her faint sleepy voice. "You know mother is washing clothes and today is your turn to help her."

"Oh yes, today is Friday. Thanks, Glenda."

The sounds created by mother only ruined nature's melodies because it brought me sorrow. It reminded me that she had a day of difficult work ahead of her. Even the freshness of the morning's air was hampered by the scents of soiled laundry and soap rising into the air.

Rubbing the sleep from my eyes, I could see from my window the motion of mother's arms moving quickly up and down against the washboard as she bent over a tin tub filled with dirty clothes. Her hair was matted and sweat already fell from

29

her brow, mixing into the water of her wash.

"I'm up, Mama; I'm coming to help you. I'll be right there." I hurried and dressed as fast as possible to avoid her calling out to me.

As soon as I was dressed, I ran from the house to join her, and just in time. She was rushing to finish the wash before the heat from the sun rose to slow her down. It was also important that the wet clothes were hung in time to meet the rising sun. Although she was exhausted, once the wash was finished I helped her adjust the clothesline that stretched about 30 feet long from one tree to another. One of my jobs was to help her place the long stick into the ground at the middle of the clothesline. This stick held the clothesline high enough to keep the clothes from touching the ground.

Now my work really began. "I have the bag of clothespins ready, Mama."

"O.K., darling. Please pass me two pins."

She picked up a dress and reached down to my hands for the two pins that I made ready to clip each end of a garment onto the line. This motion continued until the entire bundle was hung.

Boy, was I happy when mother looked down at me and smiled. There was nothing she needed to say. I will always remember the loving smile she would give me each time I helped her at the clothes line, for we were a team.

One day, hours after we'd hung the clean clothes, it began to drizzle.

"Stella, come quickly," Mama called. "We need to take down the clothes before the rain gets worse!"

I grabbed the bag of clothespins and ran to her as fast as I could.

"Do you have the bag ready to put in the clothes pins," she asked softly.

"Yes, Mama, it's right here. Remember ... we are a team."

Mother and I ran to gather the clothing from the line.

Again, I was at her side to collect the clothespins as she

removed each one from the line.

Since the clothes had been left in the sun long enough we found that they had dried, but we needed to move quickly to avoid them being wet by the threatening storm outlined in the sky. We placed the clothes into the tin tub that Mama previously used for washing. It was large enough to hold the amount of dried clothes.

As we raced to finish before the rain worsened, a sudden, strong wind began to blow. It whipped the shirts and dresses back and forth that caused them to dangle on the line as if they were dancing to the whistling and musical sound of the wind.

We finished just in time, as a sudden burst of rain began. We ran as fast as we could into the house with the clothes tub. Once again, that smile from my mother appeared! The rain no longer mattered. We were dry and could continue with our washday chores.

The next step to complete this job was to prepare the starch for ironing. I followed my mother to the kitchen as a way to remind her that I was ready to assist.

"Mama, can I help you make the starch?" I looked up at her in excitement.

"Sure, darling, I'll show you how to make it. One day you will need to iron clothes yourself." She looked down to me with her usual soft smile.

It was fun preparing starch as I flew flour into the air, onto my face, over the floor and all over my dress. I managed to spill some onto mother's feet as well. We completed making the starch by simply adding water to the flour.

"This is fun, Mama. Can I do this more often?"

"You can help me make starch as many times as you want to. Once you learn how to keep it in the pan and not all over me and the floors," mother replied with laughter in her voice.

The next morning, I was awakened by the usual melody of the chickens and birds, when I heard a noise coming from the kitchen to my bedroom. I wasn't able to identify the unusual smell in the air, but as I became fully awake, I recognized it. This was the scent coming from the steam of the iron and starch, for mother was completing the job by ironing the clothes that had been washed and starched the day before.

I followed the smell to the kitchen to watch mother as she dipped her hand into the water and sprinkled it to each area of the garment she was about to iron.

"Good morning, Mama. Do you need help?" I asked as I rubbed the sleep from my eyes.

"No, thank you, darling, go back to bed until Grandmother calls you for breakfast."

Since there was no existence of electricity in the neighborhood, the job to press the clothing called for using a heavy hot iron. Mother would place the iron over a fire on the hot furnace to heat. It was then wiped on a separate piece of cloth testing it before it touched the garment that was about to be ironed. The purpose for the testing was to avoid burning the garment.

The task of washing and ironing was completed in time to return the finished job to its owner that evening and to receive payment. Mama's earnings lasted as long as possible until the next job was received. It was a great day for ironing since the rain from the day before caused the temperature to be tolerable.

The words given by Mama that I may return to bed were well received, and I delightfully staggered back to bed.

Chapter 10—Managing Our Own Food

As there were no grocery stores in our area of Big Corn Island, we managed our food alone. We normally ate two meals a day, breakfast and lunch. On occasion, we ate Johnny cakes or rolls, and drank tea for dinner.

Breakfast generally consisted of eggs with plantains; some mornings we ate eggs and tortillas.

"Ti-Ti, could you make me a baby tortilla?" I asked, showing my baby face.

"Sure I will. I'll make you a few, Sweetheart."

"Thanks, Ti-Ti. I can't wait!"

Grandmother would make a tiny tortilla the size of a quarter especially for me.

"Is it time for me to get the eggs from the chickens, Ti-Ti?"

"Yes, but make sure they don't peck you, O.K.?"

"O.K., Ti-Ti, but they never peck me, they like me. They like how I play with them when I put a corn seed between my teeth for them to peck from my mouth," I replied.

"Estella, don't do that, you can get hurt."

I quickly ran out the door without responding.

I was happy when I was allowed to fetch the eggs from the chicken's nests. There were times I reached in a nest to gather warm eggs from underneath the hen, only I was disappointed when the nest had no eggs. But I was never attacked by the chickens when removing their eggs. Perhaps they were familiar with me since I was the one to feed them each morning.

"Here are the eggs, Ti-Ti. I found four of them, two from each nest, so warm! I hope the hen wasn't trying to make a baby."

"Thank you, Estella. I was hoping there would be enough eggs today. After breakfast, I want you to feed the chickens."

"O.K., Ti-Ti, I will."

After breakfast, I went to the yard to feed the chickens. I threw corn seeds to the ground near my feet watching the chickens flock around me, kicking up dust by their wings in their desperation for eating. Again, I held a corn seed between my teeth allowing a chicken to peck it from my mouth. I liked my crazy game and I was never injured by the chicken's peck.

Our main meal of the day was at 12 noon—the time of noon (12 o'clock) determined by where the sun shone onto our bodies. If I stood inside my own shadow, it was 12 noon. Family members often went fishing and would distribute the catch of the day amongst each other. Most popular catches consisted of red snappers and sprats. Grandmother's cooking was always delightful and she loved being in the kitchen. Her fried fish was so crunchy that the bones could be eaten along with its meat. However, when I swallowed a bone, I immediately ate a piece of bread to dislodge it from my throat.

"Today is Sunday and I think I'll make chicken and dumpling." Grandmother tested us to see what we would say.

"Yea, I feel hungry already." I said loudly.

"Or maybe I'll fry some fish."

"Ti-Ti, I like the way you cook chicken and dumpling," Glenda chimed in. "I can even help you pluck out its feathers." Glenda often offered to help.

"O.K. I'll cook a chicken. Glenda, please catch one for me."

"O.K., Ti-Ti."

Glenda went to the yard looking around. I watched as my sister chased the chickens. Finally, she made a sneaky move and caught the plumpest one she had set her eyes on. She tied the chicken's feet together with a string, carrying it upside down to grandmother.

"Thank you, Glenda. This one looks big."

"Yes, it is the biggest and I had a hard time catching it. It kept flying up and down into the air to get away from me. But I caught it. It must have known it was going to be eaten today."

A special treat was one of grandmother's chickens and she prepared it from scratch. First, to kill it she would either ring the chicken's neck or chop off its head. The most horrific memory of my childhood was to witness a chicken running around with its head cut off and blood spouting from its severed neck.

"Should I make rice and beans?" Mother asked.

"Yes, child. That would be very nice." Grandmother was happy to hear that someone else would prepare the rice and beans for it is a difficult task.

"O.K., Mother, I'll have cousin Burchel husk a coconut and maybe he will even chip it for me."

Lunch was never complete without a serving of rice and beans, although there was extra work in making this dish. To prepare the rice and beans a coconut must be cut from the tree and removed from its husk by using a machete. Using the same machete, the shell is then chipped away to reach the meat of the coconut. The meat of the coconut is grated by hand with a small grater, cutting it into small pieces that are then mixed into a pan of water. By stirring the small grated pieces of coconut into water, it releases the milk that is squeezed by hand from the trash of the coconut. Finally, the coconut milk, rice and beans are cooked together.

On occasion, if we did have dinner, it would consist of one Johnnycake (roll) and tea. We grew our own tea close to our house that was easily reached in the dark of the night. My most enjoyable tea was called Peppermint Tea. The flavor of the peppermint lingered in your mouth long after you drank it. Today, it is still my favorite tea and it often brings back fond memories. Unfortunately, there were many nights I cried myself to sleep for not having our tea and Johnnycake, so my big sister Glenda would rock me to sleep, as she took pity on her baby sister crying of hunger.

Chapter 11—Days with Big Sister Glenda

At age five I often joined my big sister for we were each other's only childhood company. It seemed that she always knew how to solve a problem and I was her constant pupil. We did everything together.

"Glenda, can I shoot down the next bird?" She was using a slingshot to kill birds for our meal.

"No Estella, you're not strong enough and the slingshot can hurt you."

"But can I try."

"O.K., I'll let you. But don't get vexed if you keep missing."

I tried and tried, but could not sling the rocks high enough. After many attempts, I became frustrated but too stubborn to give up trying.

"See, Estella? I told you."

"Can I try two more times, please?"

"Fine, but no more."

I held the pebble in the slingshot but I let go too soon. "Ouch, that hurts. The rubber came back to my hand and stung me."

"O.K. Estella, that's enough. I'll get in trouble if you get hurt. I've got a good-sized bird. That's enough for our lunch."

"Let's play house, Glenda. I will cook the plantains and you can cook the bird." I ran to the kitchen and gathered water in my toy pot and a plantain. I walked back to Glenda and watched as she burnt off the bird's feathers. Then she put the bird on a sharp stick and began to roast it over ground fire.

I started another little fire and cut the green banana into three sections. Then I put the sections into the now boiling water. Suddenly, the pot boiled over and the fire went out. As usual, big sister came to my rescue, putting my pot to her fire. The banana sections seemed to be cooking nicely, and I sat down to wait.

When I finally looked into my pot, I couldn't believe what I was seeing. "Glenda, look at my pot! The banana sections have turned blue!"

"We can't eat that. It may poison us." Glenda looked in disgust.

"I'm sorry, but I tried to make it good for us."

"Well you tried; maybe next time."

I never saw this happen again and we never found out why!

Glenda and I often arose at 5:00 or 6:00 a.m., in order to take our horse to the green pastures. Butku was very well trained, having a mild temper. He had a beautiful silky golden-brown coat that matched the color of his mane and tail and was very much loved by the family. On our way to the pastures I often traveled bare-back, while Glenda walked ahead leading the horse by a rope, but sometimes we rode together. It was fun when Glenda allowed Butku to gallop around while I bounced up and down on his back. This filled me with joy and laughter. This was our own childish game.

One morning I didn't feel like getting up so early.

"Estella, wake up. It's time to take Butku out."

"Can't you go by yourself today?"

"Yes, but we'll have fun if you come."

"O.K. But can you let Butku hop around with us?"

"Sure, get up and let's go."

A little time later, we were on our way. This was our daily routine.

A second horse, Whitie, was owned by a family member but often kept at our house. Whitie was also a beautiful horse, with his mane and tail as white as milk, but he was extremely vicious. The only person allowed to mount this horse was its owner.

Whitie was extremely smart. He often returned home alone leaving his owner to walk his way home when he stopped to converse with friends along the way.

Glenda and I stood far away from this horse to avoid being

kicked. Even Butku stayed away from him.

Family horses are not only used for traveling but also for racing, and pulling wagons with coffins to funerals and burial grounds. However, Whitie was never the one to handle such orders.

[One night, years later on Long Island, New York, while my son Eric was returning home, he discovered that our neighbor's horse had gotten away from its barn and went running down the street. Having experience with horses, Eric was able to retrieve this wandering horse and returned it to its owner. Amazingly enough, this horse's description was the same as the one we owned in Nicaragua years before. Additionally, its color was the identical brown. What was most haunting is that we learned the name of this horse was Butku. Could this be the reincarnation of our own Butku?]

Figure 14: Eric, Age 10 - In a riding competition at camp.

Early one morning while taking Butku to pasture, we noticed our new neighbors. They were identified as East Indians, who had recently moved into the neighborhood. Their house sat just next to ours. Since their arrival, my sister and I noticed the sugar mango tree was becoming barren.

The next morning, Glenda looked up at the tree and said, "Estella, there's hardly any ripe mangoes; only little green ones are left!

"I know! That boy we saw yesterday ran away with them. He had so many he dropped one from under his arms."

"Let's get up earlier and get to the tree first," Glenda suggested, as we returned home empty handed.

Those mangoes were very sweet, giving the tree its name as the sugar mango tree. It was also the only tree of its kind in the neighborhood. My sister and I soon won the mango race by being the first ones up each morning. Finally, the neighbor boy gave up the chase. He just couldn't beat us!

We also had the pleasure of a cocoa tree near our house that produced healthy beans. We used these cocoas for making hot chocolate drinks, but before we could do this we had to process the little beans.

First, we picked the pods from the limbs of the tree. We then broke open these pods exposing the sweet white coated pulp that covered the seeds. (We often enjoyed sucking the sweet pulp off the seeds.) The seeds were then cleaned and placed in the sun to dry. Once dry, they were peeled and ground into powder in a small hand mill. Finally, we added just enough water to the powder and rolled it into balls of chocolate ready for use.

Figure 15: Cocoa Tree with cocoa bean pods

Each season or month produced its own special chore. In December, we made perfume from the sweet yellow flowers grown near our house. We placed these flowers into a small bottle of water and waited a few days for it to ferment. After sampling this made-up perfume for its potency, we would splash ourselves with it and paraded around as if we were grown-ups wearing perfume.

This was more fun than Christmas, which we seldom remembered or celebrated. Santa rarely arrived at our house.

However, one December morning, I awakened my sister.

"Glenda, wake up. Wake up!"

"Good morning, Estella."

"Good morning Glenda! Do you know what today is?"

"No, what is today?"

"Today is Christmas," I reminded her but she was aware of what today was.

"I hope Santa brings us toys this time," I said as I sighed.

Glenda looked discouraged for it would be a miracle if Santa made it to the house.

"I sure hope so," she responded. "If he makes it to our house, do you know what we can do?" she asked.

"What?" I inquired.

"We can put a bottle of perfume at Mama's bed and make believe Santa left it there for her. She will like the perfume we made."

"That's silly. She'll know we made it."

"She would still be happy. It would be like Santa left it," Glenda insisted.

"But what if he doesn't come?"

"Then we can tell her it's from us."

"O.K. That is a good idea."

Although Santa Clause very seldom arrived at our house for Christmas, we understood that something had gone wrong with his plans when he didn't show up. We quickly dismissed the disappointment of not receiving Christmas presents since it was something we had grown accustomed to.

However, one Christmas he did arrive and I was happily presented with a red whistle. Upon his second arrival, I received a plastic brown and white dog the size of my hand. My sister received the best present since she was the eldest—a plastic black and white donkey shaking its head, also the size of a hand.

The following day after Christmas it rained all day long. Since walking barefoot was our lifestyle, during rainy seasons our feet became muddy, causing a fungus between our toes called "Chigger". Chigger is commonly known as Athlete's foot in the United States. This fungus caused our feet to itch uncontrollably.

One day while walking in the rain, my sister and I decided to stop at the beach to wash the mud from our feet. However, we spotted sharks just as we were about to place our feet into the waters. Normally, a storm causes the sea to lift higher, allowing sharks to rise above the reef and into shallow waters near the beach.

That day the winds blew strong and the sharks were swimming just below us where the seas splashed against the edge of the land. Once we spotted these sharks, we returned home without washing our feet. However, we were safe from the jaws of sharks.

On rainy days, my sister and I made certain that our machetes (large knives) were placed in a dark corner of the house. This was to avoid their connection with the tropical lightning storms that might cause a fire; so we believed. We then improvised on ways to keep ourselves busy.

Some games we played in-house were jacks and flipping match boxes. The goal of the match-box game was to scratch the long side and short side of the box until a white dot was revealed. We'd flip the match box into the air and if it landed with the side showing the white dot facing upward, you won a point. The game continued until one of us earned the total amount of points previously decided on to win the game.

Another fun thing to do was to fill a soda pop bottle with sugar and water. We would lie around enjoying our made-up soda and listening to the rain on our tin roof, while telling each other make-believe stories. Finally, the sound of the rain on the roof served as a lullaby that sang us to sleep.

Unfortunately, Corn Island had no electricity, and television was never in our reach.

Chapter 12—Limited Waters

Fresh water was very scarce on some tropical islands and we had our share of drought. In order to have access to water, we hauled it from the neighborhood well. This was a difficult and dangerous task since there was no protection built around the well to prevent us from falling in. One day our grandmother became nervous when she heard a yell for help.

Ti-Ti entered the house in a panic. "Stella, where is your mother?"

"She went down the street." I became frightened by the look on grandmother's face. Had there been an accident?

"I just heard someone scream for help. I need to know that it wasn't your mother. I'm going to the well!"

She rushed from the house as fast as a person of her age could move, with Glenda and me just behind.

When we arrived at the location, we saw that our neighbor's husband was pulling his wife out of the well. No one knew how long she had been there, but luckily, the well was shallow enough to prevent her from drowning.

Mother appeared in time to see what happened.

"Hettie, I'm so glad to see that you are all right," Ti-Ti cried. "When I heard someone cry for help I prayed it wasn't you."

"I'm here, Mama. I'm also glad it wasn't me. I hope that never happens to me or any of us." Mama looked at me and Glenda and smiled. "I was just down the street when I heard the cry for help. That's why I came."

"O.K., Dear. I'm just happy that you're safe."

We used well-water to wash clothes, for cleaning, and for bathing. Bathing was done in a deep tin tub, once a week on Sunday morning. It was important to bathe on Sundays before going to church.

To fill the tub, heavy buckets of water were transported by a horse. However, those strong enough would carry one or two buckets to their houses.

We didn't use well water for drinking, cooking, and brushing our teeth though. Instead, we used rain water that was caught into a large barrel. We also used this water to wash our hair.

To properly scrub our teeth a wet cloth was dipped into baking soda or ash from our stove. This is the method used for toothpaste but toothbrushes never entered into our lives. Although we maintained shiny clean teeth this was not a treatment to keep them healthy, only to keep them clean, and our mouth odorless.

On the same day as the accident at the well, Mother laughed as she announced loud enough for all to hear that frolicking at the beach would be in celebration that she had not been the one who fell into the well. "So, come on, children, let's go down to the beach."

"O.K., Mama."

I quickly ran to change my clothes but turned around sharply as I remembered to ask, "Mama, can we take Butku to the beach?"

"Sure. You and Glenda can ride him in the sea waters. He needs to cool off, too."

"I'm ready," Glenda shouted as she entered into the room fully dressed for the occasion.

When we arrived at the beach, it seemed that other neighbors had the same idea. For once we weren't the only ones there. It was a hot day so this was the place to be.

Glenda and I rode into the waters on Butku's back.

"This is fun. Giddy-up, Butku. Let's go! Wheeee!"

I laughed and laughed as Glenda instructed the horse to gallop into the refreshing sea waters. I'm sure that Butku also enjoyed the waters.

Although water was scarce in this neighborhood, we spent a lot of time at the beach that was not far from where we lived. The sea is credited for keeping us healthy, and it was believed that its salty waters were the cure to all the cuts on our skin.

Spending time at the beach served as a form of recreation. Little children loved to ride on the back of those bigger than themselves, and adults rode their horses into the sea to cool them off. The horses seemed to enjoy this treat as they galloped into the ocean and back out again, with their owners on their backs. Here, there was no limitation of waters for the ocean reached out farther than our eyes could see.

Living in such a small community meant that we got to know each other, and such gatherings at the beach always turned into a family reunion.

While at the beach we ate cocoplums that surrounded us, and were always ready for the picking. These plums grew wild but were safe to eat, and mostly grew at the beach.

As we left the beach, the cocoplums we picked were nature's way for saying "thank you for coming."

Figure 16: Arena Beach Hotel and Villas, Big Corn Island, Western Caribbean

Chapter 13—Miss Clara, A Very Special Person

At the age of five, a very special person in my life was a neighbor known as Miss Clara Barton. She was extremely kind and treated me as the child she longed to have. I could never identify her nationality; however, our family believed she was of East Indian descent. Her olive skin, long jet black curly hair, and slanted dark brown eyes also revealed the trademark of a Nicaraguan. Her constant smile showed a kindness that was always affixed to her face.

I was often invited to her house for cake, bread, or soup. I would eat just a small amount of these servings, for I would sneak a portion beneath the table and into my lap to share with my sister at home. I then excused myself from the table and quickly headed home to deliver some of my delights to Glenda.

On several occasions, I accompanied Miss Clara on her way to the stores. I was often rewarded with materials she purchased so mother could sew a dress especially for me.

Early one morning I was awakened to the smell of coffee as Miss Clara was in the kitchen talking idly with my mother. According to her appearance, it showed proof that she was about to make one of her weekly visits into town. It was also obvious that she was awaiting my appearance so that I might accompany her.

"Good Morning, Miss Clara," I greeted her while wiping the sleep from my eyes.

"Good Morning, Stella. I asked your mother if you could travel into town with me."

"Yes. And I gave permission, Estella."

"O.K., Mama. Thanks."

I dressed quickly then entered the kitchen to find the usual breakfast of tea and torte that Ti-Ti had left for me. I ate quickly, we said our goodbyes, and then we were on our way.

As we traveled through the woods Miss Clara said,

"Estella, did you know you just stepped over a whipped snake?"

"No, Miss Clara, I didn't see it."

"The reason you didn't see it is because it looked like a stick."

"Oh no, I could have been bitten."

"I didn't want to say anything to scare you, but everything is fine now."

Some snakes camouflage themselves to blend into sticks or leaves to avoid being seen, so I was not aware of its existence.

Traveling from place to place was either by foot or horseback. There were no automobiles of any kind.

****

In 1966, I returned to Nicaragua to visit and learned that Miss Clara was sick and hospitalized in Bluefields. I found I couldn't go ahead with my plan to visit her because my air flight from Corn Island was cancelled. I could not reschedule the flight either, since the time of my vacation had ended and I was expected back to work in America.

A few months after my return to America, I learned that Miss Clara was aware of my intention to visit her. As a result, she removed the photo from her passport and mailed it to me as a remembrance of her. When I received the photo, it showed proof of how special she thought of me, for she had me in her thoughts until the day she died.

Miss Clara's photo sits on top of my Bible in a place visible to me from each corner of my bedroom. I know she's in Heaven and I hope to see her again.

Figure 17: Miss Clara & Her Partial Passport

Chapter 14—Medical Treatment

On a clear day, after a week of rain that seemed to last forever, my sister and I were restless and eager to leave the house. With permission, we were allowed to visit our friends who lived a half mile away.

As we walked to their house, I asked Glenda, "What games should we play?"

"If the ground is dry enough we can jump rope."

We arrived to find our friends Naomi and Christina playing on their veranda.

"Hi Naomi, Hello Christina, what are you doing?" Glenda asked.

"We wanted to jump rope but the ground is still too wet," Christina responded with a face of disappointment.

Having nothing to do, we decided to play a game by jumping off their veranda. This was a mistake for the veranda was definitely too high for a person of my size to handle. However, I didn't want to miss out on the fun. Then, when I jumped I landed head first.

"Get up, Estella." Glenda shook me, but I lay on the ground … my eyes closed. I had blacked out.

When I came to, I asked, "Glenda, what happened?" I didn't remember anything that had happened.

"You fell on your head when you jumped from the veranda."

I tried to sit up. "Ouch. Glenda, I can't straighten up my head and it hurts a lot."

"Estella, lets walk home slowly."

"O.K., but I still can't lift up my head and it hurts real bad."

Mother appeared at the door as we approached the house. She seemed confused to see my head resting on my shoulder.

"Estella, stop playing. Hold your head up. You look silly

49

walking like that."

"Mama, she can't hold up her head. She's not playing. Estella jumped from the veranda that was too high and landed on her head."

"Glenda, you're the oldest. Why did you let her play that game? Now run and get Auntie Toya. And you're in trouble."

Glenda ran as fast as she could to the midwife who handled such medical needs of the community. On their way to the house, Glenda told Auntie Toya what had happened. She described the nature of the accident, and that I wasn't bleeding. With this information, Auntie Toya knew exactly what she needed to do.

"I'm here, Mrs. Frederick. Where is the child?"

"Please come into the dining room. Estella can't lift her head from her shoulder, but she's not bleeding."

"O.K. I'll tend to her. You just wait outside and don't come in if she cries out loud. I know what I need to do and it will hurt. But when I'm done, she will be fine."

Once Mama and Glenda left the room, Auntie Toya took my head and twisted it bringing my neck back into place. My neck had been out of its socket.

There were many times I jumped from the veranda but this time it was different. I learned the hard way that this was not a safe game to play. I also learned that my mother was a woman of her word, for I was warned not to play this game and now I was in trouble for being disobedient.

Without medical doctors, we often depend on either Auntie Toya, the midwife Miss Victoria, or the elder, Grandmother Ti-Ti. They were considered our medical group.

By living without a physician, we were on our own, but our self-made medical team did the best they could to cure our ailments. They were never paid for their services; just a simple "thank you" was enough.

Grandmother Ti-Ti was credited with saving her grandson's foot when he stepped onto a poisonous "Ping-Wing" prickle. His foot had swollen to its capacity, and turned purple, blue and red.

She mixed a multitude of ingredients then added flour to serve as a paste. Finally, she covered the area with a cloth that served as a comfrey by keeping the ingredients together. This so-called medical treatment was to prevent him from developing gangrene. Several days later the poison poured out along with green puss and his foot was cured.

The day I received a cut to my head Mother decided there was no need to visit either of this medical group for Mother washed the blood from my head and concluded that I was not in danger.

Previous to this accident, Mother had seen the rope in my hands from the corner of her eyes.

"Estella, don't you try to make a swing."

"I made it before, Mama. I know how to make it."

"If you fall I'll give you a spanking for disobeying me."

I went to the side of the house where Mother could not see me and proceeded to tie a rope to the cocoa tree where I made a swing. Shortly after, the rope became untied and I started screaming as I swung to the ground. As a result of hanging the swing, the limb broke; I flew into the air and landed head first onto a rock. And besides my suffering from the fall, I received a spanking, as promised by mother for disobeying her in the first place.

Later I decided to join my sister in making a seesaw. We cut a hole into the middle of a long bamboo stick, stood it onto a shorter (half size) bamboo stick that we placed standing upward into the ground. This was a success for the bamboo withstood our weight. Thankfully it never broke.

Playing in the bushy area of the yard for many days was very testy, for we became covered with ticks. Thankfully, they were not harmful; we simply plucked them from our skin.

Although we were poor, we didn't realize how poor we were, for this was our way of life. We made our games and lived our life. Perhaps not knowing the difference made no difference.

Chapter 15 — Those Who Wanted to Adopt Me

At the age of five, while still living at grandmother's house, a number of people wanted to adopt me. The first request was made by a one-legged musician named Zeckie, followed by Miss Clara, my Godmother Lillian and her sister Miss Pet.

Early one morning, I was told by my mother that Godmother Lillian was on her way to get me. It was only then that I became aware of this arrangement. I was told that plans were made that I may spend time away from home under the care of this person that I'd never met before, for she lived on a separate island in Nicaragua, known as the Bluff. I only knew her by name for I was just an infant when I was baptized and it was then that she was chosen to become my godmother. Since godparents are highly regarded in our culture, this would be the chosen person allowed to take me away, but just for a while.

Mother bent down and faced me gently to explain her purpose for sending me away. I was made to understand that spending time with Godmother Lillian would give me the opportunity to experience a better way of life, even if just for a few days. Unfortunately, she was not able to provide me with such luxury that I would receive from my godmother. She took my hands in hers and explained further.

"Estella, my dear, I'm letting you go with your Goddie (Godmother). You will spend time with her and you'll enjoy being there. She also wants to celebrate your birthday with you."

"O.K., Mama, but I didn't know she was taking me away with her."

Ti-Ti stood silently, not saying a word.

Suddenly, a voice called from the door — godmother Lillian.

"I'm here, Hettie."

"Good Morning, Lillian. Estella is ready to go. Please take

good care of my baby. She can stay with you on vacation for a while."

"Sure. I'll take good care of her, Hettie. I'll dress her in fine clothing and you won't recognize her when you see her again."

I said my goodbyes and we were on our way to catch the next boat to the Bluff. It would require traveling by boat far away from our home of Corn Island and I didn't know how far or how long it would take to get there. I only knew I was on my way to a place I'd never been to before, and I was extremely nervous.

I was assured that this would be the beginning of many of my future birthdays I would spend with Godmother Lillian. She explained that her retirement from the position as a midwife would allow her the opportunity to do all the things she never had time to do before. I was assured that I was not forgotten, for I was the daughter she never had. This brought a smile to my face, for now I had the pleasure of having two mothers—one poor, the other wealthy.

At this time, no one was aware of what Miss Lillian had in mind and what she was up to when taking me away. It was much later when her intensions were revealed.

Chapter 16—Returning to Godmother's Care

One year later at the age of six, I was finally returned home to my mother, dressed in a beautiful white dress and white caroche shoes. This gave the impression that I was in good hands and living extremely well. Mother was truly impressed.

The separation between the two islands gave Godmother Lillian the opportunity to keep me beyond the length of time which I was to return home to my mother. She knew that mother could not afford the expense to travel, so it was to her advantage to keep me beyond the agreed length of time.

We arrived early morning in time that I may join my family for breakfast.

"Hettie, I'm sorry I could not return sooner. But I want you to see how well Estella looks and how happy she is. With your permission, I would like to have her stay with me for a little while longer."

As mother walked with her head bent down to the floor, she paused for a moment then turned around to give her response of approval.

"O.K, Lillian. I see how well my baby is and I thank you for that. You have my permission that she may return with you for a bit longer."

"All right, Hettie. I do want to celebrate her seventh birthday. I'll return for her tomorrow morning."

"O.K., Lillian, see you tomorrow."

Mother took my hands together and gently covered them into hers as she bent down to look into my eyes, and then she kissed me on my cheeks.

As she spoke gently to me, I noticed my sister Glenda listening intently, tears rolling down her cheeks. There was nothing I could do or say to her but I knew how she felt because I

54

felt the same. We both knew that we were taught to do what we are told, no questions asked.

"Estella, I'm letting you go with your Goddie for a bit longer. I'm glad you're enjoying yourself. All right, Dear?"

"Yes, Mama."

Early the next morning I was awakened by my mother.

"Good Morning, Estella. It's 6:00 a.m. and your Godmother is on her way to get you. Go to the kitchen where your grandmother is waiting for you."

I sat up in bed, reached both hands to the skies and gave the biggest yawn anyone of my age could manage to release.

"Good Morning, Mama. I'm getting up now."

I hurried to the kitchen where Grandmother stood waiting for me to appear. A basin of warm water was made ready that I may wash-up and breakfast was in a small frying pan that sat over a warm pot of water on the wooden stove. I knew I should hurry, in order to be ready upon the arrival of Godmother Lillian. So, I moved as quickly as my little feet could carry me.

After breakfast, I sat on the veranda waiting anxiously not knowing what to expect, for hours had passed and I began to wonder if Godmother may have changed her mind.

Suddenly, my sister Glenda appeared from the back of the house to reach the front where I sat waiting.

"Estella, your Godmother is here. She's coming around the back of the house."

At this time, Glenda ran inside the house to let mother know that my Godmother was coming. Mother had walked toward the back of the house, so when she heard Glenda's voice coming from the front door she then reversed her position and hurried back to the front door. It was as if they were playing a game, for when one person was in the front the other was in the back. Finally, my mother and godmother met at the front door with open arms.

"Good morning, everyone, I'm here."

"Good morning, Lillian," Mother responded.

"Sorry I'm so late, but the banana boat was late coming from the Bluff. The captain said it was due to the roughness of the seas."

"Well, I had Estella ready for you. She has been sitting on the veranda looking out for your arrival, and seems excited to spend more time with you."

I stood excited and ready to leave.

"Good morning, Goddie."

"Good morning, Estella. Are you ready to spend your birthday with me?"

"Yes, I sure am. Are we leaving now?"

"Well, I need to check on my mother once more and then we will leave. I'll return for you. Just be ready when I return."

One hour later Miss Lillian reappeared. She walked quite rapidly toward the house, as she belted out, "Estella, we must hurry. We need to catch the next boat. It's the last one leaving today. Hettie," she yelled out. "We must go now. See you soon."

"O.K., Lillian. Take good care of Estella."

"I'm coming, Goddie. But first I'll say goodbye to Mama, grandmother, and my sister Glenda."

I turned to Glenda who was filled with emotions, for this was our second time of separation from each other.

"Glenda, I'll miss you but I'll send you something. I don't know what it would be, but I'll send you something."

"O.K., Estella. I'll miss you, too. I don't want you to go. I have no one to play with." Glenda was sobbing as I hurried to follow Miss Lillian. I hurried to keep from crying.

Miss Lillian succeeded when she tricked mother about how better off I was under her care. She received the approval needed and once again I was on my way, to leave my beloved family for the second time.

It was very sad to leave my family and as I hurried away, this time I don't know why I didn't cry. Perhaps I was already accustomed to being away for such a long time, or maybe I simply ran out of tears. However, while being away I truly missed my sister whom I was very close with since the day I was born. She was always my big sister, closer to me than my own mother. I worried about her, but knew, somehow, I would send her something to make her feel better, and someday we would be together again.

In later years, she revealed to me of how much she cried and how lonely she felt when I left home. I also learned how happy she was to receive the gifts I sent her.

Luckily, Godmother and I arrived at the dock in time to board the next boat to The Bluff. Three hours later we arrived. The Bluff was a small island that sat in the middle of the western Caribbean. In my mind, it must have been what was left over from the makings of other islands that God created with His very own hands. However, there were many people to meet and much to learn about this place that appeared to be very different from my home in Corn Island.

After we docked, the next thing was to walk to Godmother's house.

"My house is just a few steps ahead of us," reported Miss Lillian.

"Yes, we're almost there," I responded.

Leaving Corn Island, we arrived to the Bluff at dusk, probably about 6:00 p.m. Upon our arrival, I was greeted by Godmother Lillian's husband Mr. Herrero and approached by my 12-year-old cousin Dulfie, who also lived there.

"Hello, Estella," was a friendly greeting from Dulfie.

"Hello," I responded shyly.

"It's too late now, but tomorrow my friends and I will take you fishing," he assured me.

"Thank you."

Figure 18: El Bluff Port, Nicaragua[3]

The next morning, I was awakened by Godmother's call to breakfast. Dulfie was already at the table and soon to finish his breakfast.

"Estella, when you finish eating, I'll take you out in the dory (canoe)."

"I never went fishing before, but it sounds great," I responded.

After breakfast, we went to the beach where a dory was kept for travel and fishing. I helped to push the dory down to the waters and we both hopped in. Dulfie was good at steering and we went far out to sea.

The winds were blowing, the air was fresh, and the sun was smiling down onto our faces. It was a good day for fishing.

I watched as Dulfie threw out his fishing line. Unfortunately, the first fish caught was that of a mat ruse (blow fish).

"Look Estella, this one is for you. Scratch its belly and see what happens," he instructed. I scratched its belly and it blew out like a balloon. (A blow fish is simply treated as a toy. Compared to the fish eaten by the villagers, it was considered to be nasty,

---

[3] Ports.com ... seaports: info, marketplace. Photos provided by Panoramio are under the copyright of their owners.

since it ate any and everything in its path.)

We threw this fish back into the waters and continued fishing. There were fish after fish that we pulled in and dumped into a pot of water that was held ready for this occasion. Once there was enough in the pot we joyfully returned to the house. Godmother would be happy to receive such an abundance of fish, and it was obvious what the serving would be for dinner.

This was a good day, and I was sure the rest of my stay would be just as exciting. However, I was dead wrong. It was my belief that there would be much to talk about upon my return to my family back home; however, that day never came.

Chapter 17—Living with Godmother Was Hell

As time went by, living with my godmother at The Bluff was hell and I often felt alone. Seldom was there a conversation between us for she acted as though I didn't exist. My return to her the second time was worse than the first. I was made to sleep on the floor, and my main source of food was bananas, mangoes, and other fruit that I ate during the day. One morning I was surprised to be included at the table for breakfast; the bread with jam and eggs that was served to me on a small saucer was great, and it was delicious. That day was special.

On various occasions strangers delivered powdered milk to the community and I was one of many children who ran towards the line to be there before they ran out of supply. We were told that these deliveries came from a place called the States (United States of America). I remembered someone saying that the States was a rich country, where it is so cold your fingers could fall off right before your eyes if you stayed outside of your house too long. It was also a place where the streets were paved in gold, with large beautiful houses surrounded by white picket fences with green grass, and stationed on the hills. I often wondered if my father lived in such a place and if so, would he return to us and take us there.

Suddenly, while in deep thoughts of the States the voice of my Godmother yelled out. "Estella, make sure you get to the line for milk that should arrive shortly from the States."

"I will, Goddie."

While playing in the yards, I looked out to see if people from the States had arrived. At about 10:30 a.m. that Saturday morning I finally saw them setting up a table to begin their distribution. I began to run toward the line when I called out to my friend.

"Alicia, the States people are here with milk."

"O.K., I'm coming, but my shoes are falling apart."

"Why do you wear shoes anyway?"

"I don't know. Mama wants me to wear them, but I'm not used to wearing shoes."

"They look like they're running away from you. You should take them off and you'll move even faster."

"O.K., I'll take them off."

"That would look better. Hurry, let's go."

To see Alicia's shoes dangle on her feet was such a funny sight that it caused us to laugh on our way to the line. As we looked at each other we continued to chuckle during our entire way to the milk line.

Although it was expected of me to take the powered milk to the house, I would sometimes eat a portion of it on my way home, for it also served as a change of menu.

I never had the means to purchase candies or anything else from the candy store like other community children. As I watched them run around while they enjoyed their sweets, it made me feel left out and beneath them; so the consequence of which I would acquire the means to be at their level did not concern me. When I got the sign from Godmother's husband to go upstairs, I would have money to buy candy that would bring me to the standard of the children whom I played with.

I was a puppet on a string when he gave me the sign to go upstairs. The sign he gave was to place his thumb between his two fingers on one hand. I knew I wouldn't like it but I complied with his order. I can't believe Godmother never stopped this molestation that she witnessed when she walked up the stairs and saw this action. She turned around and walked back down the stairs, ignoring the situation as though she didn't know what to do, or what to say. This behavior continued from the time I was seven years old until I left at age nine.

My entire days were spent in the streets with other community children where we played ball and other games. I loved the game of baseball and became a very good batter. Team leaders often fought to have me on their team.

"I want Estella on my team," Fernando yelled out.

"No, she's my friend. I want her on my team," shouted Roberto.

It didn't make a difference what team I was on, since I so loved the game of baseball. We played until dusk but made sure to return home before dark.

Once we finished with our games I returned home where I was assigned my daily work to clean and clear off tables at the bar that was owned by my Godmother, located on the main floor of our house. The treat I made for myself on these occasions was to sneak and drain whatever liquor was left from the customers' glasses or bottles into my mouth. I was fortunate never to become intoxicated, although one day I felt a little dizzy.

The Bluff was a stop-over for seamen traveling afar, so the bar was a convenient place for them to rest, even for just a few hours before continuing to their final destination. Most of these customers were of German descent, coupled with various nationalities.

On various occasions, a seaman named Mr. Smokie often visited this bar. He noticed that I was poor and began to favor me. This gentleman was of dark complexion, extremely skinny and short. His hair was black and frizzy, with a bald spot on top of his head. He had the appearance of a happy man, always kind and courteous. Mr. Smokie treated me as if I was his own daughter and never left without asking me to dance for him.

"Estella, dance for me. I like the way you dance the Mambo," he would say.

"O.K., Mr. Smokie."

He would laugh out loud, pat his feet and clap his hands to the enjoyment of my entertainment, as I shook my hips and rolled my hands over each other while I danced the Mambo.

Often when he returned from a trip Mr. Smokie would have a present for me—a small red rubber ball, a rubber doll, a porcelain doll, and finally, a little basket with candies wrapped in red transparent paper. Mr. Smokie was the closest to being the father I had ever known. He certainly gave me the impression of what my father would look like.

I remembered the promise made to my sister that I would send her something, so I sent all of these gifts to her as I received them; with the exception of the porcelain doll, which I decided to keep for myself.

One day once school had ended, I asked my friend Anita to help me build a hammock for my doll. Since school was held at the teacher's house, we proceeded to build the hammock between the classroom windows. I was fortunate to approach her just in time before she left for home.

"Hi, Anita. Can you help me make a hammock for my doll?"

"Sure."

Once our hammock was completed we placed my doll in for a swing.

"All right. Let's sing a lullaby, too. Do you know of any?"

"Sure. Let's sing 'Rock-A-Bye-Baby'."

"O.K. That is the only one I know."

We placed the porcelain doll firmly into the hammock and sang a lullaby as we rocked it to sleep. Suddenly, a monkey flew down from a tree and startled me, as it landed onto my feet. This caused me to jerk the hammock that caused the hammock to break and the porcelain doll went flying into the air and shattered into pieces beyond repair.

I gathered each part of the doll as I sat on the floor while tears ran down my cheeks. There was a leg here and a leg over there. The eyes were separated a distance apart from each other when they rolled away as if they did not belong together. My effort to place each part into its proper place was impossible, and there I was without a toy of my own. I couldn't believe my doll baby was gone and I wished that monkey was never born!

Figure 19: The White-headed Capuchin is found in four Central American countries.[4]

Chapter 18—School Days at The Bluff

School was not a requirement at the Bluff; however, there was one school house that supplied education to the entire small island. In addition to this school, one person who offered to teach was Godmother's sister Miss Pet, who held classes at her house. This was the school that I attended, since she was considered a family member. Each morning we began our class with the pledge to the flag and sang the Nicaraguan National anthem.

Miss Pet was a very stout lady in her 50s who always appeared to be extremely stern and her disposition caused us to be afraid of her. She lived alone without a husband or child, but seemed to be quite comfortable, although her teaching was voluntary. She'd came back to Nicaragua from England ten years before, where she once resided with her husband and worked as a teacher. Following her husband's death, she returned home, where she offered to teach children in her area. This was not a paid position; however, Miss Pet was financially stable.

Her students took lessons on slates no matter how cracked they were, so memory was very important, for when English lesson was over the slates were wiped clean to learn mathematics. We were well behaved children, paying strict attention to the teacher. Of course, if we didn't, the penalty was being hit with a ruler or made to stand in a corner away from the class.

Other punishments included variations of standing on one foot, and holding up the other foot or one ear with the other hand. Another was to kneel on rice. Many boys got into trouble if their hats were not removed or when they didn't say "good morning" as they entered the classroom. If the parents found out one of their children misbehaved in school, that child would be spanked, in addition to the punishment they'd already received from the teacher.

As I sat next to my friend I noticed that her slate looked brand new and in much better condition than mine, so I bent over to ask, "Anita, is that your new slate?"

"Yes, I got it for my birthday," she whispered back to me.

"It looks so pretty. I wish I had a new slate. Mine is all cracked and the sides always come apart. I keep pushing the sides together to hold in the plate."

"Oh, Estella, I'm sorry. Maybe you'll get one soon."

"Maybe," I said sadly.

School lasted two or three hours a day, since classes only consisted of Mathematics and English. However, I knew these lessons would be of significance to support me in the future.

Chapter 19—Time Spent at the Cays

One of our usual activities was working at the Cay for this gave us more financial support. On a day in 1953, my Godmother, her husband Mr. Herrero, and her twelve-year-old nephew Dulfie and I, traveled to two very small islands known as the Little Cay and the Big Cay (we pronounced "cay" as "key".) We went over in a dory (canoe) that Godmother's husband drove, steering with a paddle.

In later years, millionaires from different countries began buying pieces of these little islands, building homes and creating their own little worlds. However, no one lived on them when we went there.

It took approximately 45 minutes to reach our destination. Our first stop was at the Big Cay where sugar cane grew and where a mill was stationed that we used to grind the canes. Our job was to make sugar, syrup, and coconut cakes that were sold at the bar when we returned to The Bluff.

Once we arrived at the Big Cay, Mr. Herrero would immediately cut down the canes in an effort to finish our work before dark, for there was much to be done in the two days (Saturday and Sunday) after our arrival.

"Estella, you and Dulfie must hurry and take the canes up to the mill. We must begin as soon as possible," Godmother would yell.

"O.K., Goddie."

"You know we must finish before dark."

"Yes, I know. I'll move fast. Goddie, can I have a coconut cake when we finish?"

"Yes, just hurry."

"Thanks."

Trips up the hill to the mill were many and extremely

difficult for a child of my age. Several long canes rested on my shoulder making climbing up the slope awkward. When enough canes were collected, they were ready for grinding.

Grinding the sugarcane stalks required three people to operate the mill. One person stood at each end of the beam to push it around in circles. This beam is attached to the top of the mill and reaches about five feet high. The mill is approximately three feet tall and sits onto a 2-foot stand. When the beam was pushed in circles it causes two large oval balls to turn, while a third person places each cane, one by one, between the rolling balls. An iron pot is stored at the spout of the mill to catch the juice as it is squeezed out from the cane. Once the juice is caught in the pot, the cane becomes trash and exits through the back of the mill and drops to the ground. The pot is now taken from the mill and placed over a fire to boil into syrup and sugar.

Once we completed this task the preparation of coconut cakes began. Coconuts are pulled from the trees, then hacked, chipped, and grated. Syrup is now combined with the grated coconut and molded into small balls, the size of a golf ball, known as coconut cakes. This completed the work of the day.

When work was done, we traveled approximately 10 minutes across the waters to the Little Cay, where there was a small shack for sleeping. The Little Cay is a bare high land with few trees, and without the existence of animals or people. It was filled with thousands of bullet shells that covered the grounds of the entire island, left from previous wars, and it was only natural to kick them around as we walked.

Several chickens were raised at the Little Cay. Where they came from I did not know but they somehow survived on their own. Unfortunately, hawks were always lingering around as I witnessed their predatory behavior when one suddenly lifted a chicken and flew away holding it between its claws as it flew into the skies.

Figure 20: Lime Cay, Nicaragua.[5]

Lime Cay sits in the Caribbean Sea, off the coast of Nicaragua, just 1.5 hours north of Bluefields. This is Large Lime Cay.

Figure 21: Little Lime Cay

Always, while at the Little Cay, Dulfie and I loved playing in the sea. We had discovered the joy of standing under the overturned dory. There we enjoyed the reflection of colors created by the sun that danced around us.

That day when we arrived Dulfie said, "Estella, help me turn over the dory."

"Great!" We turned the dory over in the water and it floated. "I'd better go under to make sure there's enough air to breathe and light to see." With this I ducked under the dory and then raised my head until my shoulders were out of the water.

Shortly after, I returned to the surface. "We have plenty of room." Then we plunged into the sea beneath the canoe.

"Oh, it's so beautiful under here, Dulfie. The fish keep swimming around us like they're playing a game. They probably think we're giants and wonder what are we doing here, but they don't seem to be afraid of us."

"I like the colors. They are so bright and so pretty. We should do this more often," he chimed in.

While we stood beneath the canoe, we admired the sunlight that danced on the waters, creating beautiful rainbow colors, and filled with images of sparkling diamonds that danced around the blue waters of the seas.

When we weren't at play by day, we were out to the sea at night. Guided by the moonlight and bright stars, we rode out to sea in the dory to catch a stingray. Dulfie stood tall in the canoe with a harpoon in one hand and part of its attached rope in the other hand. The rope allowed room to maneuver the twist and turns of the stingray in its determination to escape. It also prevented us from capsizing when the stingray dragged the harpoon beneath the dory.

Figure 22: A Stingray Underwater

Dulfie continued to stare down at the waters and waited anxiously for the reflection of a stingray to appear, that gave the moment of when to strike.

"Dulfie, I see it over there," I shouted, with nervousness in my voice.

"Where is it?"

He looked down to see its shadow and suddenly threw the harpoon. It struck a stingray the size of a standard car tire and we anxiously dragged it toward the shore. It began to shake furiously to release itself from the harpoon but without success. I moved quickly, taking the stick, we traveled with and pushing the canoe towards the land. As we got closer to the beach the stingray helped to carry our weight in the proper direction, with the harpoon still in its back.

We dragged the stingray onto the beach, careful to stand clear of its tail. It was believed that the nail at the end of its tail was poisonous so we took extra caution. Once the stingray was stoned to death my cousin collected the nail from its tail— Dulfie's hobby that I never understood.

The next morning, we gathered ourselves, drank our cup of black coffee, then headed back to the Bluff. I often wondered why there was never anyone else visiting at the Cays; we were always the only ones there.

Two days later Godmother Lillian suddenly remembered there was something she left at the Little Cay, so it was important for us to return there immediately. She explained that the coffee pot left behind was a memento given to her by her deceased mother. She wanted to retrieve it before someone else visiting there found and kept it. We immediately returned to Little Cay.

Once we arrived at the Little Cay, there was no such pot to be found. She then reported the need for her to return to the Bluff but would return shortly. Dulfie and I were told to remain there until she and her husband returned. This was unusual and I sensed that something was wrong, but could not determine what it was. We had never been left alone at this little island in the past, and her actions were very suspicious.

Chapter 20—Bringing Father's Children to America: First Stop Bluefields

In November 1953, father decided to have his children brought to him in America. To proceed with this arrangement, a letter was sent to mother convincing her of his intention. He promised that their children would receive the best of care, and proper education would be provided for them. He further explained to her that due to his employment on a passenger ship that traveled around the world, it would not allow him the opportunity to make the trip himself. Therefore, he would hire someone to represent him for gathering his children and bringing them to him.

To proceed with this arrangement, father sent a second letter to mother with details of the arrangement. He informed her that his representative Rose Taylor would arrive on a certain date and to hand over his children to her. When mother received this information, she notified Miss Maggie Valley, the keeper of Eleanor, and Lillian Walker, my Godmother, to expect this individual on a certain day, and to have us ready for immediate release to her.

We learned later that after becoming quite friendly with this lady friend, Rose, father had hired her to travel to Nicaragua, where she was to gather his children and bring us to the house he had already purchased and made ready. This new home was located in Brooklyn, New York. (Unfortunately, due to his employment, he would be abroad when we arrived.)

He told Mother that Rose was excited to carry out this task. Actually, Rose was extremely fond of our father and felt this task would give her the opportunity to have a promising future with him. It would also allow her the opportunity to travel abroad, which was something she could not afford if not offered the opportunity to carry out this task.

Once briefed, and after receiving all the necessary instructions on where to stay and who to see, she was on her way to Nicaragua.

As instructed, her first stop was to Bluefields where his daughter Eleanor lived under the care of Maggie Valley. Arriving early morning on November 2nd, Rose appeared at a house that resembled the description that was given to her. She approached the house carefully and stood at the bottom of the steps, where a lady sat in her rocking chair on the veranda.

"Hello, is this the home of Maggie Valley?" Miss Rose inquired.

"I'm Maggie Valley," was the response from a very stout lady as she slowed down the motion of the rocking chair.

"I'm Rose Taylor. Mr. Fredrick sent me. He said I should see you and you would know the reason I'm here.

"I did receive his letter. Please come in." Miss Maggie arose from her chair and led Miss Rose into her house. "I understand you will take his children to him."

"Yes. He gave me instructions of where each child would be and I understand that Eleanor lives with you."

"Well, Eleanor has been with me since she was five years old. She goes to school at the Anglican Church where her mother wanted her to continue her studies. But the States would be a much better place for the children. I'm so happy for them, and their mother always wanted the best for them as well. I only hope Eleanor will someday understand that. She's outside playing right now and I'll call her after we chat for a bit."

"Maggie, have you lived here for a long time?" Miss Rose inquired.

"Yes, this is the only house I ever lived in, since the day I was born. Let me show you where you will sleep, and then I'll call Eleanor."

"Thank you." Miss Rose put her belongings away then joined Miss Maggie. They walked to the front of the house where

Eleanor played with other children. Her black curly hair was bouncing like springs as she ran around the yard, with a slightly dirty face that came from the earth they trampled in.

"Eleanor, come here," Miss Maggie called out to her.

"O.K., Miss Maggie, I'm coming."

As Eleanor stood in front of them, Miss Maggie gave her a loving smile.

"Eleanor, this is Miss Rose. Your father sent her to get you."

"Why?" was the first response from Eleanor. She then turned to Miss Rose and addressed her. "Hello, Miss Rose."

"Hello, Eleanor. Your father sent me to bring you and your sisters to live with him in the United States."

"You mean the States?"

"Yes. The correct name is The United States of America."

"O.K., but I hear only rich people live there, and it is so cold, your fingers can fall right off your hands."

"Well, Eleanor, maybe when you get there you'll become rich, too," Maggie added. "But you should know that your fingers won't fall off. People do wear gloves to keep their hands warm," Maggie added.

"Miss Maggie, if I get rich I'll send you some money."

"O.K, Dear. Now let's go inside. You will leave tomorrow to join your sisters and to say goodbye to your mother."

They entered the house where Rose and Maggie chatted before the day was over.

Chapter 21—Bringing Father's Children to America: Second Stop the Bluff

The day following her arrival in Nicaragua, Miss Rose took Eleanor with her and boarded a banana boat. The boat took them to The Bluff where I lived with my Godmother Lillian. Directions given by people she passed made it easy for Miss Rose to find the house that was located a short distance from the dock.

As told by Miss Rose … when she arrived at the house of Godmother Lillian, she was told that I was away at the Cays and would not return for a few days. Miss Rose would not stand for such a response and it led to a heated argument between them.

"Lillian, you were told to have Estella ready for my arrival and that I would be here today! I demand that you return her to me, as her mother instructed you to do."

"Well, Rose, I don't know how I can do that since my husband is not here and he has the dory that we use for traveling. Unfortunately, you must leave without her. But you may return again when she's here."

"That will not do! Who is that man out there fishing? Does he know where the Cay is located?" She spoke with anger in her voice.

"I don't know him," was Lillian's silly response.

Miss Rose looked at the man with a small child fishing. They were a distance out to sea, but close enough to hear her call. She walked onto the edge of the concrete blockade that divided the waters from the land and yelled out, beckoning him to her. He saw the urgency in her behavior and paddled the canoe quickly toward her to find out what she needed.

"Hello, Miss. Do you have a problem?"

"Yes, I do. Are you familiar with the Little Cay, and do you know how to get to there?" Rose asked.

"Yes, madam." Luckily, this gentleman spoke English that allowed them to communicate.

"I need you to get a little girl from there and bring her to me. I will pay you $100 American dollars when you return."

"Sure, madam. I will do that for you. What is her name?"

"Her name is Estella. Please hurry."

"I'm on my way. I will return with her."

The fisherman paddled away quite rapidly to honor her request. At that time one American dollar equaled seven cordovans (Nicaraguan dollars), so this was a hefty payment he could not refuse.

While at the Little Cay, I heard someone calling my name from the beach. I ran to answer the call assuming that Godmother Lillian and her husband had returned for us. Instead, it was a stranger, and with him, I assumed was his seven-year-old son, whom I recognized from the neighborhood.

"Hello, is your name Estella?"

"Yes, sir, my name is Estella."

"Well, a lady sent me to find you and bring you back to The Bluff."

"O.K. But my cousin will have to come with us."

"That's fine. There's enough room in the dory."

My cousin and I were not in fear of this stranger, for he seemed harmless and trustworthy. We hopped into the dory and headed to The Bluff.

Once we arrived, a lady was standing on top of the hill waiting to receive us. She paid the fisherman and he left after giving a grateful thank you with a big smile on his face that was as large as the sun. She turned to me.

"Hello, Estella. My name is Miss Rose. Your father sent me to bring you and your sisters to live with him in the United States."

"Will I get to tell Mama goodbye?"

"Yes. We still need to get your sister Glenda."

"Yay! I miss my big sister."

Being left at Little Cay was proof that I was being hidden

away by my godmother, for she knew Miss Rose was coming to get me. It also showed that I had been stolen, since I was never returned to my mother after so many years. I had been with my godmother since I was only 6 and now I was 9.

When I arrived at The Bluff, I immediately recognized my sister Eleanor as she stood at the side of Miss Rose. I had been introduced to her a while back when a friend of both Lillian and also of my mother, sneaked me to visit her while we were in Bluefields. I was told to keep quiet and not to reveal my visit to my godmother. At that time, I was 7 and Eleanor was 11. I didn't know the motive of that lady or how she knew about my sister Eleanor; however, she seemed to have had a big heart and it was a very kind thing for her to do. She must have known something that I didn't know, and I don't even remember her name.

I wondered if Eleanor recognized me. However, as I approached her it was obvious that she did.

"Hello," I said softly.

"Hello, Estella. Do you remember me?"

"Yes, Eleanor. I met you one day in Bluefields. A lady sneaked me over there to see you."

"Yes. I'm so happy to see you again."

"I'm happy to see you, too." Suddenly I felt that I was not alone. I had my sister Eleanor again and according to Miss Rose, I was about to meet up with my big sister Glenda, too.

To be with my sister Eleanor again was very special, for we had been separated since I was eighteen months old and she was five-years-old. After being separated so many years, I felt that I had gained a brand-new sister.

I didn't have suitable clothing to make a trip to America, but somehow a dress was prepared for me by a next-door neighbor. A pair of shoes that Dulfie had outgrown, was given to me, although sizes larger than my feet. We moved quickly in order to catch the next boat to Corn Island to gather my sister Glenda, and to say goodbye to Mother and Grandmother. Luckily, we managed to catch the next banana boat.

One day during a conversation with my sister Glenda, it was revealed to me that our father often sent payments to my mother, and she in turn forwarded payments to my Godmother to help support my needs. Mother inquired about the gold chain he had sent to me for my birthday; however, I never received it, nor was I aware of it. I suddenly realized the purpose I was kept by Godmother Lillian, is that I was financially beneficial to her.

In later years, I learned that upon my departure from Godmother Lillian, she was in the possession of another little girl, whom she sold to a German seaman. I often wonder if that same fate could have happened to me.

Figure 23: Estella Victoria, Age 9

Chapter 22 — Bringing Father's Children to America: Third Stop Corn Island

It was November 6, 1953, when Miss Rose, my sister Eleanor and I were on our way to Corn Island to find our other sister Glenda and to say goodbye to our mother and grandmother. We were successful in reaching the banana boat in time before it left the Bluff; for it would be the last boat leaving for the day.

Banana boats were the least expensive and most dependable way to travel. These type boats are built with shelves especially made for transporting bananas, leaving little space for anyone or anything else. Since space is limited we stood on our feet while holding on to the beams around us during the entire time of our travel. It takes approximately 45 minutes from the Bluff to Corn Island, so standing on our feet was not too difficult for us to handle.

Miss Rose was not familiar with this type of transportation but seemed to handle it well. She looked down at me to check my wellbeing.

"Estella, hold on tight. I don't want you to lose your grip."

"O.K., Miss Rose. But the boat keeps rocking so hard."

"I know. The sea is very rough today," she said, then checked with my sister. "Eleanor, how are you doing?" she asked with concern.

"I'm fine, Miss Rose. I'm holding on tight."

"O.K., we should be there soon."

We landed at Corn Island in mid-afternoon and the captain gave us directions to Grandmother's house. The house was not far from the dock so there was no difficulty in reaching her as we traveled by foot. When we finally arrived to the house Miss Rose introduced herself.

"Good afternoon, Mrs. Frederick," she said to Mother. "Your

husband sent me to find his children and bring them to him in America. He said that a letter was sent to notify you that I would represent him and to expect my arrival today."

"Yes, I did receive his letter. Please come in," Mother responded.

This was a very moving day for me, for it was three years since I last saw my family and four years since I lived away from them. Therefore, to me, this visit served as both hello and goodbye.

When we arrived at mother's house, I noticed that Glenda was already dressed, and she appeared eager to make the trip to America. I went to her and whispered in her ear.

"Glenda, Miss Rose is taking us to the States to live with Papa."

"Yes, I know. Papa wants us to live with him. He wrote to Mama to let her know he will take good care of us. But I feel sorry to leave Mama and Ti-Ti."

"I know you do."

I then went to my mother and gave her a hug. She looked at me with sadness in her eyes.

"Estella, I'm so glad you will live with your father in the States. It is a much better place and you will all be together again."

"Yes, Mama." At that time, I didn't know what came over me but I began to cry, and I cried and cried. I'd never cried before.

Mother invited Miss Rose to sit while they discussed the legalities of our departure. During their conversation, Miss Rose said, "Mrs. Frederick, I want you to know of the difficulty I experienced with Lillian. She left Estella at the Little Cays to hide her away from me. I was able to pay a fisherman $100 American dollars to travel there to find her, and he was successful in bringing her safely to me."

Mother replied, "It made me vexed that Lillian kept Estella away from me for so long. She knew I could not afford to travel. But I knew this day would come. My husband told me he would one day send for the children and I'm so glad he kept his word." Mother showed anger as she spoke.

"Mrs. Frederick, here are the necessary papers you need to read and your signature of agreement is also needed." Miss Rose handed mother the papers and a pen, and showed her where to sign.

Mother looked at the papers and recognized Father's handwriting. She took the pen that Miss Rose handed her and signed the letter of agreement to make it legal.

"Here, Rose. It is done. I only want the best for the children. This is good of their father, for I know he loves his children and they will be together again. Tell him I said thanks."

"Don't worry, Mrs. Frederick, I will see that the children reach him safely."

Mother turned to each of us, showing love and concern while trying to hide the tears in her eyes, but without success.

"Estella, you must behave yourself when you're with your papa, and don't forget to visit me someday. I must stay with Ti-Ti. She's getting old and I must take care of her, so go ahead with Miss Rose and your sisters."

My final goodbye was to my grandmother Ti-Ti. I somberly approached her as she silently stood by observing all that took place around her.

"Goodbye, Ti-Ti. Thanks for making those baby tortillas for me. I will miss you very much and I love you. I'll be back to visit you."

"O.K., Dear. I know you will be happy. Tell your papa I said hello."

"O.K., Ti-Ti. I will."

Now that the final one of us was gathered, we needed to return to Bluefields with Miss Rose, where our necessary papers would be completed in order to leave the country. Not having a boat available to make this return, it was only possible to travel by canoe. To travel by canoe from Corn Island to Bluefields was extremely dangerous for it was a long distance over the deep sea.

It would take hours and prayers for us to arrive safely but with the grace of God, we survived.

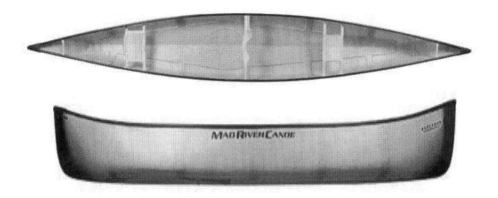

Figure 24: Dory/Canoe

Upon our arrival at Bluefields, it was agreed that we would return to the house of Miss Maggie Valley until all our papers of release were in order for us to leave the country.

Chapter 23—Credentials/Preparation to Leave Nicaragua

In order to receive our passports, it was necessary that we travel to Managua, the country's Capital, where such applications are submitted. We arrived at the Immigration Office early morning on November 9, 1953 as planned. While we stood on line Miss Rose observed a list of instructions posted on a wall that outline all that was needed to submit our application. She quickly turned to us letting us know that we may not have all the necessary paperwork. We were then instructed to stay calm and to act as though we didn't know.

When we finally reached the front of the line, Miss Rose calmly handed over our birth certificates to the clerk through the opening of the glass window.

"Good morning sir," she said, as she calmly passed our papers to the clerk. "I'm here to help these children apply for their passports and permission to leave the country." As he gathered our certificates we were scrutinized with suspicion made by his squinty dark brown eyes as he looked over the rim of his glasses. He ruffled our papers one by one then looked up with aggravation on his face.

"Where are the Police Records?" he asked.

"Police Records?" she asked.

He ignored her question then pointed to the wall. "Did you read the sign posted on that wall?"

"I did read the sign but they are only children," responded Miss Rose.

"It doesn't matter. That is the law," he responded.

"Where do I receive such police records?"

"I see on their birth certificates that they were born in Bluefields, so that is where their records are filed. Once you have those papers in order, you may return to us."

Although Miss Rose was prepared to cover the expense for the flight of Nicaragua's Lanoka Airlines, she was concerned that her finances were dwindling before her eyes. To avoid the additional expense, we remained at the lobby of a hotel while she returned to Bluefields alone to collect such records from the police department. It was easy for her to achieve this demand and later that afternoon she successfully returned to us with papers in hand. Now that all our documents were in order we returned to the immigration office.

At the second attempt to receive our passports, we were told that Miss Rose was not permitted to represent us in this endeavor, for she was not a Nicaraguan citizen. It was the policy that a person holding citizenship was the person to submit such an application. However, since my sister Glenda was sixteen years old, she met the age requirement to act as our guardian. Therefore, Glenda was granted the right to submit our applications and we successfully gained our passports, along with permission to leave the country. We were finally successful, and returned to Miss Maggie's house where we arranged our departure to leave Nicaragua.

Since we traveled with only the clothes on our backs there was no need to carry much luggage. However, the little we owned was placed into a small leather suitcase and carried by Glenda. Traveling lightly also made it easy to maneuver ourselves around should we needed to move quickly in a crowd of people.

That night we gathered ourselves, took our baths, and I was given worm medicine to remove the worms from my stomach. Most children in underdeveloped countries are filled with these creatures and I had many. The next morning, I ran to the chamber pot which was a frightful situation for there are times the worms would dangle when exiting. This caused me to yell out.

"Glenda, help!" I yelled. She ran to my assistance, as she

often did. Whenever I was in need of help, she was the one to call.

"Estella, you know you must pass those worms before we leave," she said.

"Yes, I think they're all gone. I was afraid when one didn't die, but it finally fell out."

"O.K. I'm glad they all passed out. Now let's get ready to leave."

At this time, Miss Rose's finances were running extremely low, and she needed a way to return to America. Somehow, she was informed of our distant relative, a cousin named Paul Wittica, who made frequent trips to Tampa, Florida. To request permission that we may join him on his next trip to America, we travelled by canoe to the dock of the Bluff where he was stationed. As we approached him, he recognized us as family members, which made it easy for our acceptance.

"Aren't you Hettie's children?" he asked.

"Yes. We are Miss Hetrudes' children. I know you from when you came to my godmother's bar just down the street," I responded. "Are you our cousin?"

"Yes, I am," he responded proudly. "Hello, Ma'am," he addressed Miss Rose.

"Hello, Mr. Wittica. I was told that you planned to leave for Tampa, Florida sometime today and I wondered if you would allow us to travel with you."

He wandered around with one hand to his hip, the other to his chin, while staring at the ground, then finally turned around and gave his response.

"Yes, I'm leaving in two hours. Why are you not traveling by airplane?" he inquired.

"Well, during my stay here, I encountered additional expenses that I didn't expect to have and now I'm broke. Their father is away from home since he's a seaman and I don't want to wait for him to wire the money I need. It would take too long."

"Well, they are my cousins. I'll be glad to have you travel

with us, but it will cost you $25.00 American dollars for each person and you need to show me your credentials."

"O.K. That's fair. Here are our documents."

"Also, you need to know that it will take five days to reach Florida."

"That's fine."

"Come with me and I'll introduce you to my crew. I will also show you where you and the children will bunk."

We were first introduced to two crew members as they stood outside the boat. They seemed to be standard workers of Mr. Wittica and we all acted as though we were comfortable with them; although we Nicaraguans always seem to trust each other.

He showed us around the boat and the location of the kitchen, which he called the galley. We were then introduced to the two remaining crew members as they muffled around the kitchen. Finally, we were taken to the room where we would bunk. Although it was a small area, there were two bunk beds, enough for our use. It was obvious that we had taken over the sleeping quarters of the crew. However, it was the business of the adults, for I was just a child.

Miss Rose and Mr. Wittica met for discussion about our travel. He explained to her that the ocean might become rather rough, and if she changed her mind he would understand.

During their conversation, Mr. Wittica confirmed to her that the land of Nicaragua is a place where most people are familiar with traveling by boat, so there should not be an issue with the children making such a lengthy trip. He also explained that although it would take five days to reach Tampa, he would make us as comfortable as possible.

Later that day we settled into our room on Mr. Paul Wittica's boat. Miss Rose confirmed their understanding and we were on our way to the United States of America.

Chapter 24 — Sailing Boat to America

On November 21, 1953, we were on our way to Tampa, Florida, USA. The boat was the size of a tugboat carrying Mr. Wittica, the owner of the boat; four of his crew members, and the four of us passengers—nine individuals to sail on a very small boat. However, the size of the boat did not concern me, for I was on my way to America!

We sailed five days over rough seas, high winds, and a storm. On the third day, we noticed an unusual and sudden turbulence. There was such a roughness that caused my sisters and me to cling to each other for we were extremely scared. It was also obvious that Miss Rose was as frightened as the rest of us, as she held on tightly to the pole of her bunk bed.

Suddenly, there was a loud knock at the door that caused Miss Rose to release her hold in order to respond. There stood Mr. Wittica swaying back and forth holding onto his wet jacket as it ruffled and clung to his body by the strong control of the wind. He explained that we were in the middle of a hurricane and such turbulence was to be expected, but all would be well. His orders were for us to hold on tight for soon the worst would be over. Suddenly, the door slammed shut on its own, and there was no more need for a lengthy discussion.

This frightful experience was too much for me, a nine-year-old, and I was extremely scared. I knew it was time to ask God for help, so the right thing to do was to reach for the Bible that was in our cabin.

"Glenda, maybe we should read the Bible," I said to her. Since I was not familiar on how to find a certain Scripture, I asked her to help me find the 23rd Psalm and we began to pray,

"The Lord is my Shepherd…."

Somehow, I remembered this prayer from when I was just a

little girl attending church with my mother. Today it is still my favorite prayer, for it brings back memories of our survival during a most difficult time.

When we finished praying my big sister said, "Estella, I'm glad you remembered how to pray. That was a good idea and I hope God heard our prayers."

"Thanks, I hope so, too."

We often ate in our cabin. Rice and beans was served to us only once a day. Although there was not much to eat, the small quantity of food did not concern me, since I was already used to eating such skimpy meals. I only felt sorry for my sisters and Miss Rose. Unfortunately, it was very difficult for my sister Eleanor to eat, since she suffered from motion sickness. She vomited most every day.

At one point of the journey the roughness of the seas caused me to be thrown from one end of the bunk to the other. The kitchen utensils and the pots and pans went overboard, which meant we went without food the last two days of our travel. A silly thing that remains in mind today is that of the captain, Mr. Wittica's, complaint of his shoes going overboard. It must have been his favorite pair of shoes.

Looking out from the porthole of our cabin was not a smart thing to do, for it created such a fright that kept me frozen for the duration of our travel. I felt it was just a matter of time before we would sink to the bottom of the ocean. It appeared as if we were the only ones in the world for there were no other boats in sight … we would not be rescued.

When observing the behavior of the seas, the roughness of the waves created the formation of several wide and deep letters of "U's" that caused the boat to drop in and out of its path. The waters covered the entire boat and tossed it around as though it was merely a paper boat, having no control of its own.

Miss Rose continued trying to give the appearance that she was not nervous, but my sisters were as scared as I was. I was extremely doubtful that we would arrive safely, but turned my thoughts to the prayers made to God that helped me to overcome my nervousness.

Although I was more experienced with the seas than the others, this was different. To look beyond the waters, it seemed as though it was a journey that would never end. The five-days seemed to last five years.

Then one day we finally spotted land. We stood outside our cabin where the temperature was cooler than what I had ever experienced before, but it didn't matter for we were approaching the dock for landing. The air was sweeter than ever, which made up for the five days spent in our cabin. My sisters and I looked at each other filled with excitement, not whispering a word.

I believe it was truly God's answer to the prayers from a nine-year-old that caused us to land safely, and most of all, ALIVE!

Upon our arrival to Tampa, Florida we were extremely thankful to Mr. Wittica for allowing us to sail with him. Miss Rose expressed her appreciation and said she would let my father know of his kindness.

I walked up to him to say goodbye. "Thank you very much, Mr. Wittica."

"You are welcome, Estella. Do tell your papa I said hello. And you must be a good girl.

"O.K., Mr. Wittica. Goodbye. Thank you."

After expressing our gratitude, we said a fond goodbye, but somehow, I knew I would never see him again.

Chapter 25—Arrival in America

On Thursday morning, November 26, 1953, we landed at Tampa, Florida, USA. Upon our arrival, Miss Rose followed the signs to the Emigration Office and we followed behind her like baby chicks following their mother hen. We then headed to the office where we began to process our paperwork in order to continue our travel. We presented our documents, received our vaccinations, as ordered, then waited for the next train to Brooklyn, New York. While we waited for the train, a complete stranger approached me in a complimentary fashion fitted for a child of my age.

"Hello, little girl, you are such a beautiful child. Would you care for a bag of peanuts?" He smiled softly as he handed me the bag before I could give him an answer.

"Thank you, sir," I said shyly.

The gentleman left our area but returned shortly afterwards and handed me a cup of ice cream flavored with half vanilla and half orange. This was the greatest first impression of the United States of America that I will always remember. I shared the peanuts with my sisters but they allowed me to enjoy the ice cream by myself.

The train arrived shortly after the gentleman left and I wondered if he was on the same train, but I never saw him again. It seemed as if an angel came to visit and to welcome me and my sisters to the United States, and suddenly flew away.

We boarded the train and were off to another experience, for my sisters and I had never been on a train before. We traveled for many hours to finally reach New York City during that evening. As we exited the train, I was shocked by the temperature, for such coldness was something I had never experienced before. It was even colder than what I experienced in Florida. Since the warm temperature in Nicaragua remained the same throughout the year, I expected the weather in America would be the same, for I didn't know better. *Must I live in such a cold place for the rest of my life?* I wondered.

We surely were not equipped with the proper clothing for such temperatures, for there was no such thing as wearing a coat in Nicaragua. We walked through the streets of New York City dressed in summer clothing heading where, I did not know, nor did I know how long the trip would take before reaching indoors.

Finally, we reached a place where we walked down the stairs to what seemed to lead us underground. This led to a subway train where I was again introduced to another experience, for this speeding car was even faster than the railroad we had just exited.

When we finally reached our destination, we proceeded on foot toward a building identified as our house. As we walked toward this house owned by my father, I was filled with displeasure, for the grounds were covered with leaves which gave the appearance that the streets were dirty. It was not covered in gold as expected and there wasn't a white house with a white picket fence and green grass located on top of a hill. My sisters and I evidently had the same impression, since we looked at each other in disappointment.

"This place is different. Look how dirty it is," I said, as I looked at the tall square building. (I later learned its description was that of a Brownstone.)

"Wow," was all that my sisters could say as they spoke in unison.

"I didn't expect this to be the place I was told about," Eleanor whispered.

At this time, I had much to learn for the month of November was fall season when leaves are normally dropped from the trees.

I continued looking upward as we followed Miss Rose into this tall, tall building that didn't resemble a house; at least not what I considered a house. There we were introduced to her family members that included a very plump child around my age, but appeared to be much older. Later I learned she was only ten.

"Alice, this is Estella," said Miss Rose. When introduced to this child, I felt there would be a problem between us, as she appeared to be aggressive.

"Hello, Alice." I said under my breath.

"Hi." She greeted me sharply, and I immediately realized that I had invaded her territory.

I never understood why my father supported this child, since her mother Serena also lived within our household. However, it must have been the sacrifice he felt he must make, since Miss Rose would take care of us, his own children, while he was away at work.

Her ten-year-old niece was supported by my father and given new clothing, while my siblings and I wore used clothing from the Salvation Army. We received one gift each for Christmas while Alice received an abundance of gifts. However, we were grateful for whatever we received, for it was more than what we had from where we came from. We never showed disregard toward Miss Rose's family members, for we were raised with respect and being poor was all we knew. There was never a comparison with anything or anyone else.

As we were led around the house I discovered there were four floors, a deep cellar, and a backyard. This house had running waters, tubs, stoves, refrigerators, and most of all, two televisions. People were talking and walking around in this box. There were two people fighting verbally, for they were competing for the presidency. It was Dwight D. Eisenhower vs. Adlai Stevenson.

I mentioned before that Miss Rose's entire family lived in my father's house—her mother, her adult alcoholic son Jerry, her sister Serena along with her ten-year-old child Alice, my father and now, the three of us children. Oh yes, and Miss Rose.

Miss Rose's son Jerry was ALWAYS drunk for he was an alcoholic. I've never known him to be employed, so his ability to support his drinking habit was a mystery. My sisters and I were responsible for delivering dinner to him at the top floor, where he lived and spent most of his time during the day and at night. Often when in an alcoholic stupor, he passed out in the streets, coming home late at night or early the next morning.

Once, Jerry did not return home for two days, which led his mother to report him as missing. This was different for no matter how inebriated he was, there was never a problem with him reaching home. Unfortunately, on the third day of his absence his body was discovered and identified by his mother at a community morgue, for he had died somewhere in the street. Jerry was only 35. Not much time was spent with this stepbrother, for he didn't live long enough for us to get acquainted.

My favorite was Butch the dog! Butch was a beautiful male collie about six-years-old and weighed approximately fifty pounds. His coat was light brown and there was a white patch beneath his chin. Butch was a good-tempered dog and we immediately became friends. I was awakened by Butch almost every morning when he licked my chin. This was his way to alert me of his need to go outside.

My sisters and I had much to learn about this new environment, and once we settled in we were given our individual responsibilities. Glenda was responsible for cooking and distributing dinner to our stepmother at her work place each evening. This task required that Glenda travel thirty minutes each way by train to the senior citizen's Nursing Home located in New York City, where our stepmother was employed as a nurse.

My sisters and I were responsible to care for the entire household which included: cleaning, mopping, taking out the garbage, washing clothes, and all else to do with the up keep of the house. Unfortunately, my sisters and I were operating as "the three Cinderellas" while Miss Rose's niece was rewarded with all her needs—private piano lessons, private school, all the new clothing one could ever want or need.

When I look back on those years, I often wondered why we were treated differently, but we never complained. It was obvious that coming to America was the best thing that could have happened to us. We now had food to eat, more than two dresses to wear, shoes on our feet, and we received one Christmas present each and every year. Our toilet was in-house and we now took our baths in a tub and not in a shallow pan of water. Furthermore, we had a father. Although he was hardly ever at home, I understood that he was at work, which meant he could provide for us.

Somehow, I knew that living under these circumstances would only give me strength for the future. This was not what I considered a punishment; it was an adjustment, and a definite improvement from what I had before.

I thank God for a loving father, even if I only met him when I became nine. I learned later that he was building up for the day he could raise his children properly. He did the best any child could ask for and I truly appreciate his dedication to us, his children. I truly believe he knew and saw for himself our appreciation and how much he meant to us! I only hope that he hears my voice when I thank him in my prayers at night for all he has done for us.

Chapter 26—Meeting Papa for the First Time

A few weeks later after our arrival to our father's home, we were taken to the airport to meet and greet him for the first time. We were told that he was expected to spend a two-week vacation with us. This arrangement was made in order that we may become reacquainted with each other.

We arrived at the airport early enough so that he would not have to wait for us. This we successfully accomplished, even with the hustle and bustle of heavy morning traffic. Miss Rose surely knew how to drive and how to avoid traffic, and I can truly say that she was a good driver. This was something else that I was not familiar with, for we didn't have cars on the islands in Nicaragua where we lived. However, I did experience the existence of cars while in Managua. Even on the mainland, I'd never seen a woman driver. This was well beyond my understanding.

As I stood anxiously waiting for Papa's approach, thoughts ran through my mind, visualizing what he must look like and which one of us resembled him the most. I then looked at my sisters as a tool to identify him with. This idea was a waste of time since we each appeared as though we belonged to three separate families. Glenda was dark skinned with kinky black hair, Eleanor was dark skinned with long curly black hair and I was light skinned with freckles and curly brown hair.

I considered our Papa to be a stranger, since I was just an infant when he left our mother. However, I welcomed the idea of being with him; for now, I could truly say, "I have a father."

Suddenly, Miss Rose turned to us with glee in her eyes, as she pointed. "See that man coming toward us? That's your father."

"Papa," I yelled, running to him before he could reach the

area where we stood waiting. I was the first to run to his arms and he picked me up and hugged me as if we'd always known each other.

"Hello, Estella, it's so nice to see you. I see your sisters over there. Let's go so I can meet up with them."

"O.K, Papa. I'm so happy to be with you." After staring at my father, I was able to identify the one of us who looked like him the most. It was Glenda! The mystery of who he was and what he would look like was finally solved.

He approached my sisters as in disbelief, while at the same time love and excitement was written all over his face. He hugged each one of them, then turned to Miss Rose and gave her a hug and a kiss. When I saw them kiss it confirmed to me that my father and Miss Rose was a couple, even though this was the first time I'd seen them together.

Although this was the first time meeting this stranger who was my father, somehow, I was in complete happiness for I felt as if I've known him all of my life. Although I was told that he left when I was only six-months-old, it didn't even matter; for now I had my papa again.

We headed to the house in the car now driven by Papa, where we would begin our new life together.

When the day was over we sat at our father's knees while he resumed his re-acquaintance with us. We listened to stories of his life as a seaman, which included the many countries he visited and his good and bad experiences while being there. Papa enjoyed our presence as we hung to his every word, some of which were extremely educational and some were simply fairytales. His stories were quite interesting, especially the ones of the mermaids he encountered while at sea. We were truly entertained when told of these mermaids, for his description of them became quite visible in my eyes, especially the one who winked at him. I wanted to believe this fairytale was especially directed to me as a story fitted for a child of my age although my sisters showed enjoyment as well.

Later we were informed that the purpose for his move to America was to make a better life for himself and his family. We were made to understand that our father's much too long absence from Nicaragua was the cause for the separation between him and our mother. Unfortunately, I was too young to fully understand the explanation of our parents' separation; however, I could only listen to his story. At this time, he shared with us how happy he was that we were all together again.

Finally, we were surprised to learn of our father's future arrangements on traveling to the Grand Cayman Island where our now sixteen-year-old brother Orlando still resided under the care of our grandfather. To bring Orlando to America would be the final gathering of his children, and his son would only make this reunion complete. It was also Papa's intention to take Miss Rose with him where she would visit the place of his birth and meet his entire family. I was again filled with excitement, for now I would meet the brother I had never known, since we were separated when I was just an infant. And I wondered if we would even look alike!

Chapter 27—Bringing Our Brother to America

In 1954, Father and Miss Rose travelled to Grand Cayman Island to get our brother Tomas Orlando. Eleanor and I were left under the care of our eldest sister Glenda for two weeks until they returned.

Living under the care of Glenda was a catastrophe since she didn't know how to cook American food. Each day we asked what was for breakfast, and what was for dinner, although we knew it would be the same—cold cereal for breakfast and white rice for dinner. However, she did the best anyone could ask for, and we truly appreciated our big sister.

Life continued as usual while our father and Miss Rose were away. Glenda placed a clock before me each morning so that I should finish breakfast in time for school; our homework was done; and the house was kept clean as usual.

One day, Glenda announced that she was making soup for dinner. This was a welcome surprise, even if it was canned soup. It seemed an eternity waiting for Miss Rose and my father to return. We wanted to resume our normal menu.

Two weeks later my father and Miss Rose returned home with our brother. I considered this as our first meeting since I was just an infant when my brother and I were separated. He was now seventeen and I was ten. Unfortunately, we didn't know how to address each other as we were complete strangers.

Eventually we became fond of each other, but were still quite distant due to our age difference. It took being in each other's presence a few months before we gained a brother and sister relationship. In later years, we all grew into a complete family and somehow developed closeness. When Orlando introduced me to anyone, he referred to me as his "baby sister", and that made me feel special. Today, I'm still known as his baby sister.

Figure 25: My brother Tomas Orlando, Age 17. Family always called him Orlando.

Although Orlando was unable to complete high school prior to leaving the Cayman Island, he attended night school after arriving in America where he achieved this goal. Following graduation from high school, he dove into studies to become a seaman.

Papa wanted his son to work on shore, but once Orlando's mind was made up, there was no stopping him. He wanted to follow in the footsteps of his father, and other male members of the family. After graduation, he applied for a position on the SS Constitution, the passenger ship where our father was already employed.

Later, Orlando was employed in various positions within the "shipping" system, finally reaching his goal as a fireman, placing him into the Engine Room. This position was extremely stressful for his duty was to operate the heating system, holding its temperature in the correct level to avoid a fire.

In 1965, he was drafted into the Army, holding a position in the Petroleum Division, where he remained until his discharge in 1968. After completing his assignment in the Army at Fort Totten, Queens, New York, he returned to work, where he was employed on the original Queen Elizabeth, a famous passenger ship of the Cunard Line.

Orlando continues to live a comfortable life with his wife, two daughters, and one son.

Chapter 28 — Attending School in America

Immediately after our arrival in the United States in 1953, my sisters and I were registered in the public-school system. I attended classes at Public School (PS)-11, located in Brooklyn, NY, where I was, according to my age, assigned to the 4th grade level. On my first day, I was given a tour of the school by my teacher. She introduced me to her peers letting them know that I had just arrived from Nicaragua. It was obvious to me according to their actions that they had never met a Nicaraguan before. However, I felt the love and attention that was given to me.

Once in the school system, it was time to confirm the level of my education, and that I had been placed into the correct grade. Since I was from a foreign country, there was no way of knowing my level without me being tested.

The method used to confirm my education was that on several occasions I was called on to read. This was done in a polite manner that allowed me to feel comfortable, for it was obvious that I was extremely shy.

"Estella, please read page five," instructed my teacher.

I walked to the front of the class immediately, while trying to control the butterflies in my stomach. I began to read, hoping the class would understand my accent.

"Sally walked in the rain wearing her yellow rain coat and yellow umbrella......"

"Thank you, Estella. Here is a cookie for reading so well."

I was often given a cookie (Vanilla Wafers) when I finished reading and somehow, I became "teacher's pet". Today, when passing these cookies on the shelves of the grocery stores, they truly evoke fond memories of my first days of school in America.

Not being accustomed to the school system, I somehow landed on the free food line during our lunch period. I did not realize this special line was to service underprivileged children only. Finding that the American food was not of my liking, I decided to give it away to those who sat around me. The green pea soup, along with a peanut butter and jelly sandwich, were unbearable, but the sweet bun and milk were quite enjoyable. Unfortunately, when my stepmother arrived to take me home for lunch, I had already eaten.

At this school, I gained many friends. I believe that by offering my lunch to them may have had something to do with it. However, they made me feel happy to have so many friends of my own age. Luckily, my foreign accent did not cause a rejection.

During my attendance, the school's Health Department thought it was unnatural for a nine-year-old girl to weigh only forty-nine pounds, so my weight became an issue. Due to their concern, a school nurse was assigned to visit my home on a regular basis to follow the progression of my weight gain.

Each month a very dark-skinned lady wearing a white dress, white stockings, and white shoes appeared at my house. Even her name was Miss White. I later learned that she was the school's nurse assigned to my case. I often wondered why they weren't concerned about her weight, since she appeared to be quite skinny herself, much less for a person of her age.

Although I was now in the United States where food was of abundance, I would still consume the amount of which I was accustomed to while living in Nicaragua. As I noted earlier, in the last three years while living with my Godmother, most of my food intake consisted mostly of fruit. Since the amount of which I ate at the table was from the size of a saucer, it was only natural that my weight would be an issue. I also needed time to acquire a taste for the new American food, as well as the intake required for a healthy lifestyle.

Each morning a clock was placed on the kitchen table before me that pointed to the time I should finish eating. Miss Rose was convinced that this would be the answer to my finishing the meal, in order to leave home in time for school. My sisters continued their encouragement but it would take some time for me to develop a proper eating habit.

One morning I noticed tiny worms floating in my cereal. Thankfully, that morning I was allowed to skip breakfast.

The next year I was promoted to the 5th grade. When I entered this class, I discovered that my new teacher's surname was the same as mine. This led my classmates to believe she was my mother. As we walked home together in the same direction it convinced them even more. Although I tried letting them know we were not related, they were not convinced. However, at such an early age, it didn't matter. This was the most enjoyment of my early school years in America.

Walking home in the snow was a new experience and extremely difficult. I would often fall as I did one day, when I landed on top of my umbrella, a very unusual way to fall … on top of an umbrella.

The next few years I was promoted along with my class, and finally to the 6th and 7th grade to begin classes at a new school: PS-45. Once I completed these grades I was again transferred to a different school: PS-117, for grades 8 and 9.

During 8th grade I became teacher's pet and was assigned to carry the section sheet from class-to-class. This sheet entrusted to me listed the names of students expected to arrive at the next class. Luckily, there was never a problem with children cutting classes.

Finally, I was somehow accepted at Prospect Heights High School, an all-girls school where I completed grades 10, 11, and 12. This turned out to be a school where white children alone were readily accepted. A few black girls were already in attendance when I arrived.

Since being popular amongst my classmates, I was elected class president for grades 11 and 12. Thankfully, I never experienced a problem in having friendships with black or white students, and during my entire school years I never observed a fight between them.

I gained many friends, was involved in various school activities, and my attendance at swimming classes was something to remember. I was once saved from drowning when the teacher reached a long pole out to me. I hung onto the pole while she successfully pulled me to safety.

I left this school in great harmony. My school mates were the greatest and I will forever wish them all good tidings and many blessings!

It is my opinion that the teachers were high-class individuals, who encouraged us to follow the laws of the land.

Fortunately, the years have changed for the better, allowing black and white students of this nation to live together in harmony. May God bless those students and teachers whom I had the pleasure of meeting in my lifetime!

Finally, on June 26, 1962, I graduated from Prospect Heights High School.

****

In those years, black students were directed to take classes assigned to them, not the classes they applied for. Although I requested stenography (shorthand) so that I could become a private secretary; I was assigned to "office practice" instead, meaning that the highest position I could attain in an office would be in the typing pool. I made the most of these classes, however, and became one of the best typists—I won the typing contest of the entire school.

During the last year of high school there was space left on my assignment card that allowed for an additional class. Therefore, I chose stenography. Unfortunately, by not having the required two years of stenography, I was not allowed a "Commercial diploma." Instead, I received a "General-Commercial" diploma.

To rectify this lack, following graduation and at the ending of each work day, I attended night school, in order to complete the additional year of stenography classes. By achieving this goal, I became the private secretary to a vice-president at J. Henry Schroder Banking Corporation in New York City, thus elevating my status to the position I had studied to achieve. There's more than one way to skin a cat!

Chapter 29 — The Mean Stepmother

In 1956, our father and Miss Rose became husband and wife. It appeared as though I was watching this movie for several years but always afraid of what the ending would be. It was clear to me that this woman's scheme had finally reached its fruition. She was now in the position to reveal her true identity.

Whenever father showed favor to any of his children, Miss Rose was sure to come between them. She wanted him all to herself. She was the leader in this family and wanted us to know it!

Life was difficult with her. I've read fiction stories about such individuals, and felt those stories were a reflection of her. If father showed love toward our brother, he was accused of showing favoritism toward his only son. To keep peace between them, father turned toward Glenda, as she was his firstborn daughter. Miss Rose then accused him of giving Glenda special treatment, since she was the firstborn daughter and who resembled him the most. He then turned toward his second daughter Eleanor, whom he was accused of showing special treatment due to her beautiful long black curly hair.

Finally, I was disliked severely, since she felt I was a reminder of his first wife, our mother. I resembled her the most. What made matters worse was the bullying I endured from her, due to my light skinned complexion and the freckles on my face. She described my having freckles in this way: "You were standing outside a screen door when someone threw out piss where I was standing, and it landed in my face."

What she did not know was that I had inherited my freckles from my Irish Grandfather, Livingston Downs! I love my freckles for they are the only reminder of our grandfather. Unfortunately, we never owned a photo of him.

One day my favorite jacket—given to me by my father—suddenly disappeared. Later I discovered that Miss Rose had given it away. She said that she gave the jacket to a six-year-old boy who had never spoken, but did so when she'd given him the jacket! I knew her story was fictitious but I only listened, not revealing my true feelings. I definitely did not believe her story. The jacket had been the most beautiful blue silk unisex jacket with an American eagle on the back. I will always remember it. I may have worn it two times only.

My siblings and I realized that the reason Miss Rose brought us to our father was to gain his hand in marriage. It was also a way to receive expensive items such as a Lincoln Continental car, and a large house big enough to hold her entire family. We learned that previously she had lived in a 2 x 4 apartment in an underprivileged environment in Harlem, New York.

My siblings and I never showed disregard toward her or her family members, for we were raised to respect our elders. Also, we remained grateful for being brought to a better place than where we came from.

One other strange thing Miss Rose did was try her best to persuade our father to insist that we call him Dad and not Papa. That was too difficult for us to handle. We continued addressing him as "Papa" until the day he died. She couldn't take that away from us.

Chapter 30 — The Move to Queens, New York

In 1962, during Father's time at home, everyone, including his wife, was on their best behavior for he was an extremely stern man. However, my sisters and I were always happy to have him at home for his presence demanded stability within the household.

This would change once he returned to work for then our stepmother would conduct gambling parties during the nights, where there was always a distribution of alcohol. The following morning after these parties, my sisters and I were responsible for cleaning up the area. This was difficult for we were surrounded by the rank smell of whisky and cigarettes left on the tables. However, we were obedient. We did what we were instructed to do.

We never revealed to our father about these events and I often wondered whether or not these parties were given with his approval. However, there were never such occurrences while he was at home.

Although these gambling events kept us awake, luckily enough they took place on weekends and not during the school week.

When he was home, Miss Rose made certain to keep our father close to her side. Perhaps she hoped to avoid giving us the opportunity of revealing any of her secrets. She maintained her position with him by fabricating stories she built against us that always caused friction within the household. Her insecurity continued to be overwhelming.

Unfortunately, the behavior of Miss Rose's family never changed either, for their jealousy of us never ended. I surely understood that our existence was threatening to them, for they acted as though they were now in second place.

Often times our belongings went missing, never to be found again. Miss Rose's sister and her niece were responsible; however, we never revealed this to anyone. We simply ignored them and kept their mischief to ourselves. It became obvious to us that our coming to live with our father only ruined the support he had given to Miss Rose's entire family.

My sisters and I were never allowed access to the telephone to call our friends. Then I learned a trick from a telephone repair person ... how to make the telephone ring on its own. From then on I was able to make the telephone ring then immediately call a friend. Everyone thought I was receiving the calls. I could talk to my friends any time I wanted using this trick, which saved me the embarrassment of never returning their calls.

Several years later our father finally scheduled himself another two-week vacation. Normally, he would be at home only two days a month once his employer, the S.S. Constitution returned to its dock. Since his vacations would normally last one week only, it was a mystery when suddenly he did not return to work within that period of time. We felt there must have been a reason for this change but we only wondered why.

One day the mystery of father's two-weeks at home was revealed. He surprised us with his plan to relocate the family to a beautiful house in Queens, New York. Suspiciously enough, Miss Rose's sister Barbara decided to move to the same neighborhood. It was believed that our stepmother contributed to the purchase of her sister's house with the support of our father's unknowing financial help.

My siblings and I were never accepted as visitors at Barbara's home. Her threatening remarks to her daughter Alice were: "If they are allowed entry within these walls, you will be removed from the premises."

Although we were now residents of Queens, but because I only had three months left to graduation, I continued attending the school in Brooklyn. In order to continue my attendance there, I was dropped off by Miss Rose on her way to work. After school,

I returned home alone by subway.

The day I graduated not one of my family members was in attendance. To observe others being congratulated by their family members made for a sad and lonesome day. I successfully graduated and returned home alone.

Chapter 31—First Employment

In March 1962, I was interviewed for hire by a foreign commercial bank located in downtown New York's business district. There I was accepted for employment to begin once I graduated from high school. This position was held four months after my interview as promised, since the date of my hire was scheduled to begin on July 2nd, following my graduation on June 26th. I accepted this position as a personal present for my 18th birthday—June 17th.

I began my first employment with this organization as a Clerk Typist in their Cash Department, where I became close friends to most of the employees. My discovery of being the only minority within the entire department was never a problem, and my first boss Hershel, whom I learned had a crush on me, was of German descent. Knowing he was attracted to me was the cause that other fellow employees often teased him, but always in a humorous way.

"Hershel, don't you think Estella and Henry would make a good couple?" was a question asked by a male employee, as a way of tormenting him about his feelings for me.

"No," Hershel responded sharply.

The Henry they referred to was a Black gentleman employed in an adjacent department.

I never paid attention to such teasing; however, many others in our office were aware that he had a crush on me. A few months later Hershel approached me to be his girlfriend, claiming he would leave his wife who lived in Germany, if I asked him to. My response to him was a simple "NO," for I would not come between a husband and wife.

Even at 21 I was naive and this led me to accept an invitation I shouldn't have.

"Stella, would you like to go with me for dinner after the Christmas party?" The one asking was one of the bank's vice presidents.

Not suspecting he had anything else in mind, I said, "Sure. Where will we go?"

"Let's go uptown. I know of a very nice place."

"O.K," I responded. I felt honored, since this was the Vice-President whom I saw as an extremely handsome man.

We took a trip uptown on the "A" train. People watched us closely for in those days, blacks and whites did not travel together as a couple.

As we entered the upper-class restaurant, we were not stared at for being a mixed couple, as experienced during our travel. The dinner date was very nice, and his conversation was of great interest, for I found him to be knowledgeable and extremely interesting. Thankfully, the trail of liquor—Manhattan's—he lined up for me did not affect my soberness. I had learned a trick to staying sober ... I always drink milk prior to an event where liquor was being served, I had done this prior to the Christmas party, and it worked tremendously well. It also helped me realize what his intentions were.

When dinner was over it was already late at night and time to return home. While heading to the train station, this gentleman stopped in front of a hotel that we were passing.

"Come on," I said. "Why are you standing there?"

There was no response, just a stance while puffing on his extravagant pipe.

"Let's go. I need to take a train home, it's late." There was still no response as he stood still in front of the hotel, while holding his pipe at hand between his lips waiting and hoping that I would join him.

Finally, I walked toward him, took the shopping bag he carried on my behalf, and left him standing in front of the hotel in zero-degree temperature, while I wore his warm scarf around my neck—he allowed me to wear it because it was such a very cold night. However, I continued walking toward the train station for I was on my way home, in the cold, in the dark, and all alone.

Once I arrived at home, I successfully sneaked into my house at 4:00 a.m., without awakening any family members, and by dodging the ramification of facing my strict father, who had been at home from one of his lengthy travels.

The next work day, I gracefully returned the scarf in an inter-office brown envelope by an office messenger. Later, I was complimented by this individual for standing up to my character. I was NOT fired!

Chapter 32—My Return to Nicaragua, The Land of My Birth

Throughout the years away from the place of my birth, the urge to return became stronger and stronger and I decided to do something about it. To fulfill this void in my life, I decided to return even if by traveling such a long distance alone. So, on Thursday, October 20, 1966, at the age of twenty-two, I was on my way back home to Nicaragua, in effort to visit my mother and other family members I'd left behind.

This trip would require that I travel via Pan American Airlines to a connecting flight in Panama on Friday, October 21st, to finally reach Managua, where I would board a third plane, the Lanika Airlines, in order to reach my final destination of Corn Island. Unfortunately, the airplane arrived in Managua too late to board the final connecting flight, so I thought. It was to my surprise when I discovered that such flights to Corn Island are only scheduled to depart from Managua on Mondays, Thursdays, and Saturdays.

Being unable to complete this travel arrangement, I then ordered a taxi to drive me into town, where I would register for a one-night stay at an unknown hotel that was suggested by an airline employee. There I would stay in order to continue to my final destination on the following Saturday, October 22nd.

Upon my arrival at the hotel, I found the desk clerks to be quite friendly and accommodating. I was surprised to find that my speaking English did not hamper our conversation, for they all spoke English as well.

After registration, I was escorted to a room where I would spend one night only. This hotel was different from what I was accustomed to, for the rooms contained a simple latch on its door, the walls were separated from the ceiling, and the sink and toilet were located down the hall away from my room.

Once settled in, I decided to explore the area, for my interest was to discover what the capitol of Nicaragua was all about. Since my appearance was that of just another Nicaraguan, it gave me the comfort needed to travel within the community. However, as I walked into a jewelry store, my American-developed accent was discovered immediately, causing a surge of their store personnel to gravitate directly toward me in an effort to make a sale. After just a while, I left that store to continue exploring the area.

While walking around town I discovered a perfect store according to their window of advertisement and lovely display, which convinced me to stop in. When I finally entered, a sparkling gold watch caught my interest, so it was my decision to purchase this item as a souvenir for my boyfriend back home. A few moments later, a well-dressed gentleman approached and introduced himself as the store manager. He suggested that I should make payment directly to him and he would have the item beautifully gift-wrapped as a special favor for me.

"Oh, that's all right," I responded. "Once I reach a final decision I'll make payment directly to the lady at the counter. I'm in a hurry and my brother is outside waiting for me." This was a fictitious story in effort to convince him that I was not traveling alone. We communicated in Spanish, the language I seldom spoke but understood well enough to respond.

Immediately after our conversation this individual walked quite rapidly out from the store, and it was only then that I was convinced that he was a robber. Thankfully, his plan to rob me did not work. I don't know how I became aware of his trickery but I wasn't taking any chances.

When I disclosed to the store personnel what had happened, it was confirmed to me that the man was a thief and the dirty old man strolling around, who I assumed was a thief, was the store's detective. This store detective had his eyes focused toward me assuming the thief and I were together.

I was asked to sit down, and then presented with a beverage as a means to calm me down. It was my opinion that they were more nervous than I was. As we chattered for a while, a lady employee felt as if she knew my family and wondered whether or not we were related, for she herself once lived in Bluefields. I only wondered if this was another relative, but kept such thoughts to myself.

Shortly after, the store detective was given instructions to accompany me back safely to the hotel. His conversation during our travel was extremely comical, as he described how he would punch out an intruder by showing his fists in motion. I smiled at his demonstration, for it seemed that I would be the one to protect him, since he appeared to be in his 70's and quite frail. However, I enjoyed his company and humorous conversation.

The next morning, I was on my way to Corn Island. As I presented my travel arrangement at the counter, an airline representative showed concern once he saw my name. He revealed to me that my suitcases were left in Panama and had not been forwarded to my final destination. This was a concern, since my traveler's checks were left into the suitcase for safe keeping.

"Miss Frederick, we received a message that your suitcases were still in Panama." he said sadly. I see that you're from Bluefields, and I recognize your name. I believe we are related. I will surely look over the arrival of your suitcases and send them to you in Corn Island. Please tell your mother that Harry at the airport said hello."

"Thank you very much! And I will certainly tell my mother you said hello." (At this time, it seemed to me that everyone in this country must be related, for the assumption that we were related also came from the cashier at the store.) Luckily, I traveled with a carry-on suitcase that remained in my possession in case something like this should happen.

Although I planned to appear in Nicaragua as a surprise to my mother, she became aware of my arrival prior to my reaching her home. I later discovered that children who stood around at the airport heard my conversation as to whom I was to visit and ran ahead to let her know to expect me.

As I questioned a stranger of the direction to mother's house and what method of transportation would get me there, I noticed a nice-looking gentleman with blond hair and blue eyes, who was listening to my conversation. He approached me in his kindness and offered to drive me in his jeep to my mother's house and all I needed to do was to give him a photo of myself. So, I did. This gentleman was gracious, as he explained that his original home was Montreal, Canada; however, he had fallen in love with Nicaragua and made it his new-found home.

When I arrived at my mother's house she was hanging clothes on the clothes line. Her hair was matted and she appeared to be extremely poor. To see her there brought back old memories of my childhood days, when I often accompanied her to place each clothes pin at her hand to complete this task. I stood quietly and after simply saying "hello," I suddenly began to cry. As my attention focused solely on her, I was not aware that I stood on a mountain of ant hills. My feet became covered with red ants that were attracted to the sugar cane trees where I stood and the pain created by these creatures caused me to cry even more. In addition to such depressing circumstances, the one thing that bothered me the most was the fact that my mother lived in a dirt-floor house.

(These houses are built with bamboo sidings, tied together with tree vines. The ceilings are covered with banana tree leaves and the floors are nothing but dirt packed down heavily and covered with sand.)

Figure 26: Tree House

Children who stood around asked why I was crying but I didn't expect them to understand. As they stood by I decided to hand out an abundance of items that I carried especially for those who lived in the area. As I distributed candies, pencils, and writing papers they thought it was Christmas all over again. Shortly after, I was taken to my grandmother Ti-Ti, where she lived in a shabby boarded house and where I would stay during my visit. Also living with her was my cousin Alicia and her four children.

Although I was overwhelmed from this unexpected experience, it was great to see my mother, and grandmother; and also to meet my five-year-old half-brother Sheridan Anastasio for the first time (named after their president Anastasio Somoza).

When neighbors discovered who I was, they pointed toward me as they uttered "that's Kookaburra." I was surprised that after so many years, they remembered my pet name that developed by me singing the same song whenever I was asked to sing. It was always "Kookaburra." Words of this song: "Kookaburra sits on an old gum tree; merry, merry king of the bush is he. Laugh, Kookaburra laugh, Kookaburra gay your life must be."

Upon my arrival at Grandmama's house I presented to her and my mother a number of gifts that included undershirts, sewing needles, threads, scissors, soaps, and toothpaste, for I knew such items were much needed, and I was lucky to have brought them in my carry-on suitcase.

The very next day while sitting around and reacquainting myself with my grandmother, a messenger arrived at the house, as he was sent by the Canadian man to inquire if I would accompany him to the movies. I said, "No, thank you." The messenger then asked if he could take me to the movies. Again, I said "No, thank you." Although it was very kind of these gentlemen, I had only one interest in mind and that was to visit my family that I had missed so dearly. Thank God, these strangers never returned.

Two weeks later prior to the last week of my visit, the two suitcases arrived showing pieces of clothing hanging on the outside, but the travelers checks were still neatly hidden in the slot as originally stored. The additional gifts of pencils, writing papers, and a child's play cape were included. All items arrived in time for distribution, which made everyone extremely happy.

Each day my mother visited us by walking over rocks across the swamp waters, which served as a shortcut to reach grandmother's house. Good balance is a requirement for taking this shortcut, and I often used the same direction to and from their place of stay, as well as to the beach.

Traveling to the beach with my cousin Alicia, her four children, and my baby brother was a delight. The cocoplums grown there reminded me that I was home again, when I examined their taste as I often did when I was a child. The coconut tree that had fallen created the perfect background for a photo as it appeared like a giant fan behind me. Children rode their horses into the seas as they floated onto the waters, giving the impression that they were gliding on air. The winds were sweeter than ever as I twirled around looking up to the skies while the air blew through my hair. If I could only store away such beauty nothing else would matter.

I was home again!!!!

Figure 27: Estella Victoria - At the beach on Corn Island, 1966

Another reason for my return to Nicaragua was to visit my dear friend Miss Clara once more before she died as she was up in years. Once I learned that she was hospitalized in Bluefields I knew it was important to visit her there, for it might be the last time we would ever see each other again. Unfortunately, the airplane scheduled for this travel was cancelled for some unknown reason and I never got to visit this dear friend. Later, after my return to America, I received a nice letter that included her photo. This photo was torn from her passport, giving the assumption that she would no longer have the need for this document. Somehow, she had learned that I tried to visit her, but without success.

As I mentioned previously, Miss Clara was like a second mother to me, for she treated me with much love, as if I was the daughter she always wanted but never had. A few months after my return to America I learned of her death. May Miss Clara Booker Rest in Peace.

The last week of my visit passed quite rapidly, and leaving the family was sad, for I didn't know how long it would be before seeing them again. It was clear to me that it was the last time I would be in the presence of my grandmother for she was already up in years; in her 80's I assume. Saying goodbye was extremely difficult and all I could do was cry, cry, and cry even more.

On my return flights to America, I checked into the same hotel in Managua where I had stayed previously. Upon my return to this hotel, there were a number of young adults staying for the night, in order to dance for the President of Nicaragua the next day. I was invited to join them; however, I declined their gracious offer, since I felt there was a chance that I might oversleep the next day, causing me to miss my flight back home to America. I did catch up with them in my dreams.

On the day of my departure I realized that my funds were running low so I decided to have the taxi driver stop at a bank on my way to the airport. Unfortunately, since there was no space to park he drove around in circles to wait for my return. After completion of my bank business I almost stepped into the wrong taxi. It was a miracle that my driver arrived blowing his horn, to keep me from making this mistake. By stopping at the bank, I was placed in danger of missing my flight; however, and the taxi driver drove 90-100 miles per hour to the airport. Unfortunately, I placed myself in this predicament since the bank opened at 8:30 a.m. and my return flight was scheduled to depart at 9:00 a.m.

When we finally arrived at the airport, I gave this nice driver all of what I had in Nicaraguan Cordoba's, including American dollars, which were many. I didn't have time to count, but he made out pretty well, since one American dollar equaled seven Nicaraguan Cordoba's (dollars) at that time. I know in my heart that I made this gentleman very happy; then I was on my way back home to America, and back to my place of employment.

During the years I was away from Nicaragua, there were wars and more wars that made it difficult for my return. However, in 1978 our mother was brought to America by our brother Orlando, and she died on December 30, 1988, after spending ten precious years with us. May Our Mother Rest in Peace!

Chapter 33—Death of Two Loved Ones

When I got home from Nicaragua, I returned to my place of employment, J. Henry Schroder Banking Corporation, right on schedule. While employed at this company I sat at an area where I was visible to the public, so men who appeared at the counters often flirted with me from a distance. Although I was very shy, Joseph was the person who gained my attention for I was attracted to him as well. He appeared to be a classy kind of a guy, handsome, with grey eyes, brown wavy hair, and about 6'4" tall.

Joseph was responsible for depositing his employee's checks into their account at the bank, which meant he came in on a regular basis. In order to gain my interest, each time he returned I was presented with poems he had written that were handed to me by the tellers at the counter. When I read these poems, they revealed to me his intelligence, and the depth of his interest in me.

Soon after, he invited me on a date, which caught me by surprise. Our first date was to his parent's home for dinner, and to meet his two sisters as well. He had a classy family and I was just as impressed with them as I was with him. It was at this time that I learned from his mother that she was requested to bring to his place of employment a brown envelope that he had forgotten at home. She discovered later that it was NOT related to his job, for it was filled with poems he had written for me.

After dinner, we attended a show at the Apollo Theatre in Harlem where we enjoyed the performance of an African entertainer, Miriam Makeba. Although this was our first date, Joseph appeared to be serious about me and I was definitely infatuated with him.

However, in just a short while I became aware that he had a drug problem. I was successful when I convinced him to seek treatment at a facility to overcome this dreadful habit. His parents were overwhelmed with joy that he agreed to honor my request, for they had tried on several occasions but without success.

One evening I promised to make dinner for Joseph, so we met each other at the train station where we boarded the A-train to his place of residency. While on our way to his apartment I asked

"Joseph, what do you want me to cook for dinner?"

"How about fried chicken, potato salad, and a vegetable? But we need to stop at the supermarket."

"O.K. No problem."

We went to the nearest supermarket, which was across the street. This was rush hour and cars were everywhere, speeding by. We needed to be careful, but Joseph started to step off the curb.

"Joseph, watch out for the cars!"

He turned to me and grinned. "We all have to die sometime. If I died, I could see my family and friends at my funeral, and I would be in the corner watching them. But I wouldn't want you to come."

But he did wait and we finally made it across the street and bought what we needed at the market. We hurried to his apartment for I needed to begin the preparation of this meal as soon as possible, for it would take a while to finish. As I stood at work in the kitchen, Joseph unfolded the folding TV tables and placed them at the couch where our meal would be served. He then placed a number of Miriam Makeba albums onto the stereo.

Dinner was a success, and we listened to music as we ate. Shortly after, and as I finished my meal, Joseph excused himself and went to the bathroom.

Due to my exhaustion caused by a strenuous work day, and of a 90-degree temperature in New York City, I fell asleep as I waited for him to return. When I awoke, the record was turning around and around for it had ended and Joseph was not in sight!

I went into the bedroom in search for him but he wasn't there. I continued into the bathroom where I found him sitting onto a closed toilet lid asleep, or so I thought. But then I noticed that his chin hung heavily against his chest. I placed my face to his nose. It was cold! Joseph was dead. I picked him up and dragged him over the threshold to the bedroom for that was all I could do. I was not aware of how I got the strength to do so, since Joseph was already dead-weight and quite heavier than I was. Back in the bathroom I then noticed the drug paraphernalia as they floated around in the waters in the sink and I knew the cause for his death.

Shortly after, and on the same day when Joseph made the statement that "we all have to die sometime," he died. I often wonder if a person is able to foresee their own death.

I rushed to call his parents and then an ambulance. The medical personnel arrived, pronounced him "DOA," (Dead on Arrival) and took his body away. His parents arrived as quickly as possible but too late to see their son's body as it was carried away.

Joseph died of a drug overdose approximately three months after we began to date, and before the chance to make the adjustment he had promised me to do. Soon after we dated we realized our love for each other and became an item, and shortly after, he was dead. We enjoyed the short time we had together and I trusted his words that he would seek help, but unfortunately, he didn't live long enough to receive a cure. Those damn drugs took my love away from me.

When I arrived at home from Joseph's apartment I was in big trouble with my father for my involvement—in my father's words—"with a druggie". Father became physical when he lashed out at me with a belt, which caused me to lose the cross that I wore around my neck that Joseph had given me. My cross was lost forever and so was Joseph, my beloved. I never found that cross.

Due to the altercation with my father, I called my friend

Louise to request approval by her mother that I might spend a few weeks at their apartment. I was granted permission to move in that night, so I packed my clothes into brown paper bags and left in the rain, in the dark, onto a train, then onto a bus to Brooklyn.

While in the middle of this trip, I endured the problem when the bags became wet by the rain that caused the clothes to fall onto the wet ground. It was quite a sight to see as I scrambled to regain the clothing from the wet ground. However, I welcomed the strong rain that night, for it was my belief that when it rains after a person's death, it was a good sign from Heaven; and boy, did it rain … it rained all night long! Luckily, my friend Louise appeared at my house to assist me in such a lengthy and gruesome travel.

A few days later Joseph's funeral took place and I ignored his wishes that I should not attend. Upon my arrival, I placed a cross made of red roses onto his casket; for he had given me a necklace with a cross, and now I've given him one in return, although in a different fashion, and for a different reason.

Two months later after Joseph's death I decided to call my sisters, for I had never been away from them before and I truly missed them. I was surprised when my father answered the telephone. He asked that I return home as he expressed, with sadness in his voice, that he would not be so difficult in the future. Later that week I returned home to the open arms of my father.

Being away from home was an educational experience, for I was able to build a bank account for the first time. This was possible since my job earnings were not depleted by the hefty financial contributions I made to our stepmother. Although I was not required to give rent payments, I took it upon myself to do so. Also, there were often times I assisted by supplying the household with various necessities, as well as gifts presented to Miss Rose on various occasions. In later years as I matured I realized that it was my attempt to win her love.

Although I was only away from home a short time, I learned a lot. And by losing my Joseph, I believe I found myself. Now at the age of 22, I looked forward to building a future for myself, and perhaps someday to have the honor of raising a family.

That year, Clinton, my previous boyfriend, also died. He was my first love at the age of fifteen when I began to learn the existence of, and the meaning of "romance". Unfortunately, Clinton committed suicide after returning from serving in Vietnam as a soldier. His body was found on the third electrical rail of the subway train. This was extremely shocking for we only began dating shortly before his departure to the army. However, death is something that came much too soon for a person who never experienced the loveliness of life.

May They Rest in Peace!!

Chapter 34 — Engagement

In 1963 while at a friend's neighborhood party, I met Brandon, a fine young man who was very interested in getting to know me better. I certainly considered him to be a nice guy, who also gained my interest in him. We exchanged information and soon after we became an item. Things moved quite rapidly, for in six months' time we were engaged.

During our engagement, I discovered that Brandon's family owned the only printing company in Port of Spain, Trinidad (West Indies) ... he was a millionaire there. In order to assist his parents in the operation of their company, he was attending business classes in America. Taking these classes would give him the ability to operate this organization in the fullest manner his parents wanted. Although I found him to be a fine gentleman; his financial status did not impress me.

One year later following our engagement and after completing his schooling, he returned to his home in Trinidad. His intentions were to have a house made ready; for this would be our place of residency once we were married. It was also necessary that he remain in his country in order to continue his position in the family's business, for he was considered to be the chosen child responsible to run the company after his father's retirement.

While Brandon was away, there was enough time for me to reach an honest decision on whether or not I would marry him and move to a foreign country. I then realized all the reasons I should NOT continue toward this marriage.

1) He looked too young, more of a child than a man.
2) I would need to move to a foreign country I knew nothing about.
3) I thought it would be a disservice to my father after all he

had done to bring me and my siblings to a better place.

4) This marriage and the move would separate me from my father and my newfound siblings after finally being together again.

5) I was simply not in love with him.

Prior to Brandon's return, my final conclusion was to call off the wedding. Unfortunately, this decision was difficult for him to handle, so he returned home to Trinidad with a broken heart that led him into an alcoholic behavior. Fortunately, his family was able to help him turn his life around. This I learned through friends who knew him very well.

After ending this relationship, I returned to my original lifestyle.

Chapter 35—Death of My Best Friend

My best friend Louise and her mother were very religious. Although I was not of their denomination, I often accompanied them to their church in Brooklyn. Louise and I often sang spirituals for I was familiar with the music of her church.

While in high school, we belonged to a singing group with three other girls, and often sang on stage. Our place for rehearsal was the girls' bathroom for our voices reflected from the walls and gave the most beautiful harmonic sound anyone could ever ask for. One day while at rehearsal, we were reprimanded by a teacher to turn off the radio. It wasn't a radio; it was just us girls having fun singing while on our lunch break. This was funny to us for we didn't realize we sounded so good. We became popular in school, and were admired as rock stars. However, once school was over, we went our separate ways.

On Sunday mornings, I often attended church with Louise where she was a member of their choir. I was fortunate when she received permission for me to join them on their trip to perform at a church in South Carolina.

On the way to their performance our travel became quite dangerous for we ran into difficult weather conditions. It caused us to arrive at 10:00 p.m. instead of 6:00 p.m., the expected time of arrival. We were surprised to find that the church remained filled with their congregation as they waited for our arrival and the presentation went on as planned. It was only then that I discovered the popularity of this choir.

Once the performance was over, it was very late and, under such weather conditions, too dangerous for us to return to New York. The congregation realized this dilemma and took it upon themselves to provide housing for the choir of approximately forty members. We were separated into groups and driven away by various church members who offered our stay for the night. I was quite surprised to see how pleasant and thoughtful these church members were to allow us strangers to spend the night at their homes.

One fine elderly couple offered to let us, Louise, her five-year-old niece, and me, stay at their home. This couple showed us around their house that allowed us to feel quite comfortable, and then we were shown to the room where we would sleep. The next morning, we awoke to the aroma of sausages and eggs, for Mrs. Thomas was busy in the kitchen preparing our breakfast. Louise and I sincerely thanked this gracious couple for their kindness, while accepting their invitation to return to visit whenever we pleased.

Soon after breakfast we were driven to the church where the bus waited to collect our entire group, then headed us back home to New York.

One day about six months later, in January 1967, I received a dreadful call from a classmate. She asked if I had heard the shocking news about my friend Louise. This classmate informed me that Louise was dead. I immediately asked if she was hit by a car, the only reason I felt this could have happened. I was then informed that Louise was murdered.

I learned that Louise decided to move away from home to live with two of her girlfriends. It was reported that returning home one night, she was followed by a stranger who shoved himself inside the house as she opened the door. Later that night her two friends arrived at home, saw blood on the floors, and traced it to a closet. As they opened the closet doors Louise's dead naked body fell out right before them. She had been raped and killed.

In an article about her funeral, reported by the newspapers, the church was crowded with more than 600 people. Her special hymn, "Showers of Blessings", was sung by a choir member whose voice sounded exactly like Louise's. It was chilling to hear

... as though Louise was singing her own song of farewell.

Now, many years later, I still wonder if she should have turned to me as I turned to her at my time of need. Could I have saved her life? Only God knows. I can truly say that she is in God's hands. May Louise rest in peace!

Saturday, January 14, 1967—B

Seize Suspect In Nude Girl Slaying

Figure 28: Article About Louise's Death

600 At Victim's Funeral

By GEORGE TODD

The suspect in the brutal murder of 23-year-old Louise ▉ whose nude body was found stuffed in a basement storage closet a week ago, was in police custody this week to await a hearing on a homicide charge.

Detectives of the 77th Squad identified the accused killer as Anderson McManus, 39, unemployed, and purported to be a drug addict. McManus has a history of 13 previous arrests on charges of possession of narcotics and burglary.

Chapter 36 — The Much-Needed Vacation

In 1967 after much depression of my friend's death, and many strenuous work days at the bank, my co-worker Nancy and I decided to reward ourselves to a vacation trip to places we had never been before. Our choices for this getaway were Puerto Rico and St. Thomas. These locations were very popular at the time, and described by our travel agency as safe, warm, and friendly.

On a cool and rainy day in Queens, I arrived at JFK International Airport's Pan American Airline tunnel three hours prior to the scheduled departure. I stood where Nancy and I had decided to meet for approximately one hour before I saw her walking swiftly toward me.

"Hi, Stella, here I am."

"Great! I've been here an hour. I wanted to make sure not to lose time in traffic, since it's a rainy day. Let's check in and find our gate."

"O.K., Stella. I'm so excited. Let's gooo!"

We reviewed our flight information, while filled with excitement as we approached the designated check-in desk for departure. We then followed instructions handed to us that guided us to the appropriate gate to await our boarding instructions.

Finally, after one and a half hours, the announcement was made for a number of designated passengers to get in line for boarding. With additional excitement, we complied with these instructions for our vacation was about to begin.

Once we entered the airplane, we found our seating arrangements to be quite acceptable, since it was of our choice to sit nearest to the wings of the airplane, should there be an accident. Once all passengers were seated, the plane lifted into the clouds. Nancy and I then decided to celebrate and ordered a tropical drink, the Piña Colada. We enjoyed our flight that was very smooth and gentle, as we discussed our plans to visit places and things to do, as suggested by our brochures.

Three-and-a-half hours later, on a Monday afternoon, we arrived in San Juan, Puerto Rico. We selected a taxi cab from several lined up with their engines running. The taxi drove us to the Hotel Americana, where we planned to stay for the duration of our vacation. This hotel was highly recommended by the travel agency. It was located within the heart of town, also, right off the beach.

Upon our arrival at the hotel, we were checked into our room and rushed to shower, dress in our finer clothing, and headed out to begin exploring. This was a short vacation that would last six days only and we didn't want to miss anything.

At about 6:00 p.m. we went to a hotel where we watched a live stage show as we dined. We enjoyed these dinners at various extravagant hotels, since we were fortunate to receive tickets through our travel agency at an affordable price. It also allowed us the opportunity to attend some of their high standard shows that included Sammy Davis, Jr., and Mel and Vickie Torme. These entertainers were extremely popular at the time.

We enjoyed these shows that were quite different from what we were familiar with back home in New York; or perhaps there were places such as these that we were not familiar with, nor able to afford at the time. So, we decided to make the best of this style of living and to have fun. We named ourselves "The Two Cinderella's of Hollywood."

One game I played at dinner was to lure the waiters to our table by holding up a cigarette to attract their attention. A waiter would hurry to our table and a produce a cigarette lighter as a courtesy to light my cigarette. Little did they know that I was joyfully playing a game!

"Oh, thank you so much," I said as the waiter stumbled toward our table. When he left, I whispered to my friend,

135

"Nancy, did you see how fast he appeared with the lighter?"

"Yes, I sure did. Now I'll take out my cigarette."

Suddenly, when Nancy presented her cigarette, the ritual was repeated. We were enjoying our own show.

The next day, another exploration on our agenda was to attend a horse race. While filled with excitement, I decided to place a $2.00 bet on a horse that I knew nothing about. Although I never expected to win, I did. This was indeed an experiment, for I didn't know what I was doing. I'd never attended a horse race before. I became even more excited for this was real; it was not a television story. My bet became a $1.00 winning, for the cost of my gamble expense was $2.00 and I won $3.00.

One night while staying up late, I took a chance to gamble in the casino of the hotel. I decided on a gambling experiment as I approached the roulette table for a play. There I won $40.00 due to the fact that my chips continued up and down for the duration of time before the game finally ended. This event began at 12:30 midnight and lasted until 3:45 a.m. Finally, I was requested to accept a last pay-off as a winning, in order that the workers might leave for the night, and I accepted.

The next morning Nancy and I danced around like children who were just let out of a cage. We danced on top of the beds, and around the room wearing towels tied around our bodies and around our heads, while singing our joyful songs. We then ordered breakfast in our room as though we were rich and famous. Later, we decided to leave the room to wander around the area.

A few days into our stay at the hotel, we became aware that the doorman would often move quickly in order to hail us a taxi cab. This was his intention in order that we may tip him for such a favor. To end this trickery, we decided to walk away from the hotel in order to hail our own ride.

One day we decided to go sightseeing, so we checked out the hotels nearest to us. As we entered the El San Juan hotel, we found it to be quite different, but appealing.

"Look Nancy, there are trees growing in the ceilings," I remarked.

"Wow, I've never seen that before," she responded.

"This place is beautiful, but I wonder if birds ever lay eggs up there," I questioned.

The ceiling that was filled with leaves and bushes seemed extremely inviting to the birds, and that was a concern of mine, since I was afraid that one would plop on my head; however, it was extremely beautiful.

During our travels, we met two brothers from Spain. One brother was a lawyer, the other a Matador. They were also visiting this great island, and invited us to the beach and then to dinner. We accepted their invitation, for they were quite friendly; however, we knew we needed to be careful of strangers. After careful thought and to avoid a situation, we decided it would be our first and final meeting with them.

The next day our telephone rang and rang. We knew these gentlemen were trying their best to reach us for another date; however, we ignored their calls. Hanging out with these two was not our intention. Besides, we still had too much exploring to do. Furthermore, there were enough interesting men in the U.S.A. for us to meet when we returned.

One day we took a small shuttle airplane for a visit to St. Thomas. This had also been included in our travel plan. As we waited at the airport for our departure, I purchase a bottle of soda from their vending machine. As I reached for the bottle, the extra change of coins that continued to fall from their soda machine must have been a way to say "thank you for coming".

While in St. Thomas, we explored the shops, ate at their diners, and visited the lovely beach, where we admired the tall trees growing in the sands. To explore this island even more, we ordered a cab for a tour. We enjoyed the island's beauty as we admired the hills, blue waters, and the friendliness of its people.

Finally, it was time to depart from this beautiful island. At that point, I experienced another welcoming surprise. I was presented with an extra bottle of rum from the store owner. That was quite nice of him, since it was free of charge. Surprisingly enough, I was allowed to carry this additional bottle over the amount permitted, without paying duty at the airport.

St. Thomas will always remain within my mind and my heart as one of the most beautiful places that I have ever visited!

Two days later it was time to return home to New York. We said our farewells as we took pictures with the hotel workers as a fond remembrance of them. Then we were on our way to the airport and back home.

Our return to work was quite rewarding, for Nancy and I were close friends with the entire department. However, soon after our arrival, we were faced with an unfortunate event … a fire broke out in our building. Nancy and I, along with other friends, decided to stop at a restaurant just across the street from our place of work, to observe the excitement of the firemen as they rushed to the building. We sat at the windows of the restaurant as they moved quickly, dressed and ready, in effort to put out the fire. It was as if we were watching a movie while enjoying every moment of it.

During their effort to save the building, it was only proper for us to raise our glasses to the firemen as they quickly approached such danger. After a few hours of enjoyment and not knowing whether or not the fire was out, we decided to return to the office to check out the situation. Upon our arrival, we discovered that the men/our fellow workers were sitting at our desks in effort to handle our assignment. They quickly removed themselves from our desks once they saw us, while appearing to be extremely happy upon our return, for they weren't the greatest typists on earth.

We returned to the office at about 3:15 p.m., approximately three hours later, when suddenly a fellow worker shouted out to me saying…

"Stella, Mr. Price (our boss) was looking for you. He was planning to throw water on you while you typed the checks." We all had a hearty laugh about this joke, and then we returned to work.

Our fun continued after we returned from vacation, for approximately fifteen of us employees gathered at a bar/restaurant after work each Friday evening. Our tables, along with hors d'oeuvres, were made ready prior to our arrival, for we were always expected to be there. Our male colleagues would cover the expense of the checks, for they believed it was the gentlemanly thing for them to do, so it was a free ride for us ladies. We enjoyed our laughs at our happy hours, and about 10:00 p.m. we dismissed ourselves and returned to our individual homes for the weekend.

Employment at this organization was a great experience and the best thing that could have happened to me, for I will always hold these employees deep in my heart!

Chapter 37 — Finding Myself

In 1968, I became interested in the entertainment field. I approached John, a colleague at the bank with this idea and we decided to explore the possibility of creating a professional singing group. We successfully gathered two additional members, George and Michael, to join us. Since I was the only female in this group, we chose to call ourselves "Stella and the Fellows".

In effort to become more polished in this field, it was necessary that we meet each evening after work for rehearsals. Since John lived in Manhattan closest to our place of employment, we agreed that his place was the most convenient for conducting our rehearsals. We began at 6:00 p.m. and ended at 10:00 p.m.

Once we developed into a sound group, we felt strong enough to approach a professional in the business for an audition. We were successful in meeting with a musical producer, but unfortunately, he voiced his opinion that the men were not of his interest. However, the female (me) did capture his interest and he requested that I return for a second audition.

As requested, I returned alone and after singing a few tunes, I discovered that this gentleman was not interested in my voice, for he had something else in mind. This became evident as I was chased around the piano, a story I often heard about, and now I am at liberty to say that this is a behavior that women in this business truly experienced. I immediately left the building never to return again, for it was obvious that he was interested in my body and I was NOT for sale.

A few weeks later, we finally discovered an additional female to join the group. Margaret had the voice we were looking for. It was clear to me that my voice was not the one to lead this group, so it was great to have found that special person needed to carry us through. Once we discovered this additional member we needed to rename the group, so we became "The Spices".

We, The Spices, performed in various places, but after a good length of time, and for no uncertain reason, we decided to go our separate ways. It was clear to me that we were not making progress, but at the time, it was a fun thing for us to do.

My being a member of this group only convinced me that it would not be my choice of employment in the future, and that I should remain in the work field of the bank where I was already employed. Having had the opportunity to experiment in show business only confirmed for me that I was most comfortable working in a more-subtle environment, and it only assisted me in finding myself.

Chapter 38—The Failed Marriage

In April 1968, I was approached by a neighbor to participate at an annual community event. This gathering was to benefit the underprivileged children in their pursuit of a higher education after high school graduation.

I was to model an American style swimsuit, and later appear in a yellow gown long enough to cover the floors. The band was helpful as they played the tune "Yellow Bird" that fit the occasion quite perfectly. I strolled across the floors and around the stage giving the appearance as though I was floating on air. I was simply having fun.

At this event, there was a band hired for entertainment. I was approached by their lead singer Jimmy, who wanted to know me better. He was definitely interested in me and I was infatuated by him. Jimmy introduced himself to me and we carried on a conversation as if we had always known each other. He then asked if I would join him at an upcoming event and I agreed.

Shortly after, I was invited to several of his functions and our constant companionship led us into being a definite couple. This bond resulted in a marriage, and shortly after I became pregnant.

Unfortunately, my pregnancy was the reason I was absent from his performances, so the night I appeared, we were both in for a surprise. The lady cuddled-up with him at his table was also surprised. He introduced me to her as his wife and she smartly removed herself from the table. Later, my husband and I planned to meet at a diner with friends just across the street.

I was stunned to see that this lady also arrived at this diner. Unfortunately for her she was standing at the opposite side of the door that I pushed open, knowing she was there. I grabbed her hair and to my surprise, her whole wig ended up in my hands. She flew to the floor scrambling for her belongings and all "hell" broke loose. The owner of the diner rushed out with a long knife held high in his hands warning that the police was called and they're on their way. As the sirens approached us, it was time to leave. We successfully departed without further incident, nor arrest.

The following year of 1969, we became parents to a beautiful baby boy, Eric Anthony. Unfortunately, due to my husband's position as an entertainer, I was often left at home alone to care for our infant. One night while he was at a function where he was hired to perform, I decided to spend the night at my father's home. This was due to the fact that my husband would not return until the next morning, leaving me alone for the night. At this time, I was simply afraid of being left alone in an unfamiliar neighborhood, so I decided to sleep at my father's house.

Later that evening I received a telephone call from my husband. We confirmed my original plan that I would spend the night at my father's house, to avoid being at home alone. As he confirmed that I would be away from home, his tone of voice only revealed to me that he was up to something, and my female intuition took over. Therefore, after our telephone conversation, I requested that my father drive me and my two-month old infant back home.

When my father began to ask "Why was I—" he simply stopped in the middle of his sentence, for he saw the look in my eyes and somehow knew the answer to that question, so at 12 a.m. I was returned home.

When I arrived at our apartment, I found our wedding photograph removed from its position and hidden in a drawer. I further noticed that our baby's bassinette was shoved away and hidden in a closed closet. It definitely appeared that our place was that of a single person's apartment.

Surely enough, at 4:30 a.m., I heard the voice of a female along with my husband as they climbed up the stairs. They were surprised to find me at home, standing at the top of the stairs, with the appearance of a crazy person, and it was obvious that I had ruined their "good night" together. This led my husband and me into a physical altercation.

"Oops," I remarked as I tore off the beautiful white suit he wore at his performances. The rollers flew from my long hair and his company quickly removed herself from the premises.

Fortunately, my female intuition allowed me to confirm that my husband was not to be trusted. Previously, his behavior was always that of a single person; however, the proof was all that I needed. Once his behavior was revealed to me, that morning I left, never to return again. It was the ending of an ugly relationship, so my decision was to terminate the marriage immediately.

That morning I moved to my father's house and shortly after, I filed for divorce. Things moved quite rapidly, for due to his absence from our court session, I was granted my final divorce. This expense I happily covered by myself.

A while later, knowing he was not accepted at my father's house, his only decision was to give up trying. I refused to communicate with him and we never saw each other again.

Friends encouraged me to file for child support but it was not of my nature to do so. It was also my belief that to harass my ex-husband to cover his responsibilities would only lead to many headaches and it would simply be a waste of time. However, I was determined to give my child the best of care and to raise him in a decent environment, even if by myself.

In order to meet my goals, I attended night school immediately after work. With the grace of God, I accomplished this task, which allowed me the advancement to a higher-level position as a private secretary within the organization. I remained employed there for fifteen years. My commitment and determination gave me the financial support I needed, in order to provide for me and my son independently.

Luckily, I was fortunate to find an appropriate baby sitter who was recommended to me by my sister.

Now at the age of twenty-five I knew it was time that I

become serious about my future. My first marriage was a failure that taught me a lesson.

Chapter 39 - The First Time I Met John Shivers

On July 10, 1971, I met John Shivers where I shopped for carpet at the store he managed in Queens. As I flipped through the carpet samples, a salesman approached me to offer his assistance. I explained to him that I was simply looking. Once he learned that I did not plan to make a purchase, he returned to his desk.

Suddenly, John, the Manager, noticed my dismissal of his employee. This was his cue to leave his seat in effort to convince me to make a purchase. I explained to him that I did not intend to make a purchase at this time. He acted as though he didn't hear a word I said and continued his walk toward me. I explained to him that I was attracted by his display of colors; however, I promised to return at a later date.

This gentleman then turned his attention to my eighteen-month-old son.

"Hello, son. What is your name?"

"Eric."

When John and Eric met each other for the first time it was love at first sight. This I observed by the special attention they reflected to each other. It gave the appearance that they had already met. Then in a very calm manner, John turned his attention to me.

"So, do you see anything you like?" he asked.

"Yes, but I'm flying out to the Cayman Islands tomorrow for a two-week vacation, so I prefer to postpone such an expense until my return."

"Well, what area did you plan to carpet?"

"My living room."

"Have you decided on a color?"

"I'm thinking of a green, shag-type carpet."

"Well let me show you what we have that may be to your liking."

He took notice of my constant handling of an individual carpet sample that I moved back and forth in my hands. Suddenly, he placed padding onto the floor, placed the green carpet sample on it, and asked me to step on it.

As I stepped onto the sample, it was obvious that the color combined with the softness of the padding was quite appealing.

"It certainly looks and feels good, so I promise to return when I'm back from vacation."

"I understand that," he said. "However, if you decide this is what you want, you may leave a deposit for your return. You only need to leave a $10.00 deposit and I will hold it for you at the current sales price; otherwise, the cost may rise by the time you return."

"I can do that. Thank you."

John was very patient in displaying various samples in which I was interested. His assistance was extremely helpful, so I left the $10.00 deposit, for he had succeeded in getting me to make a purchase. I left in a daze holding the copy of an order that I had not anticipated placing at that time. I had the idea that this ten-dollar deposit was the beginning of a something. Was this an introduction to my future, or was I seeing something more than what it was?

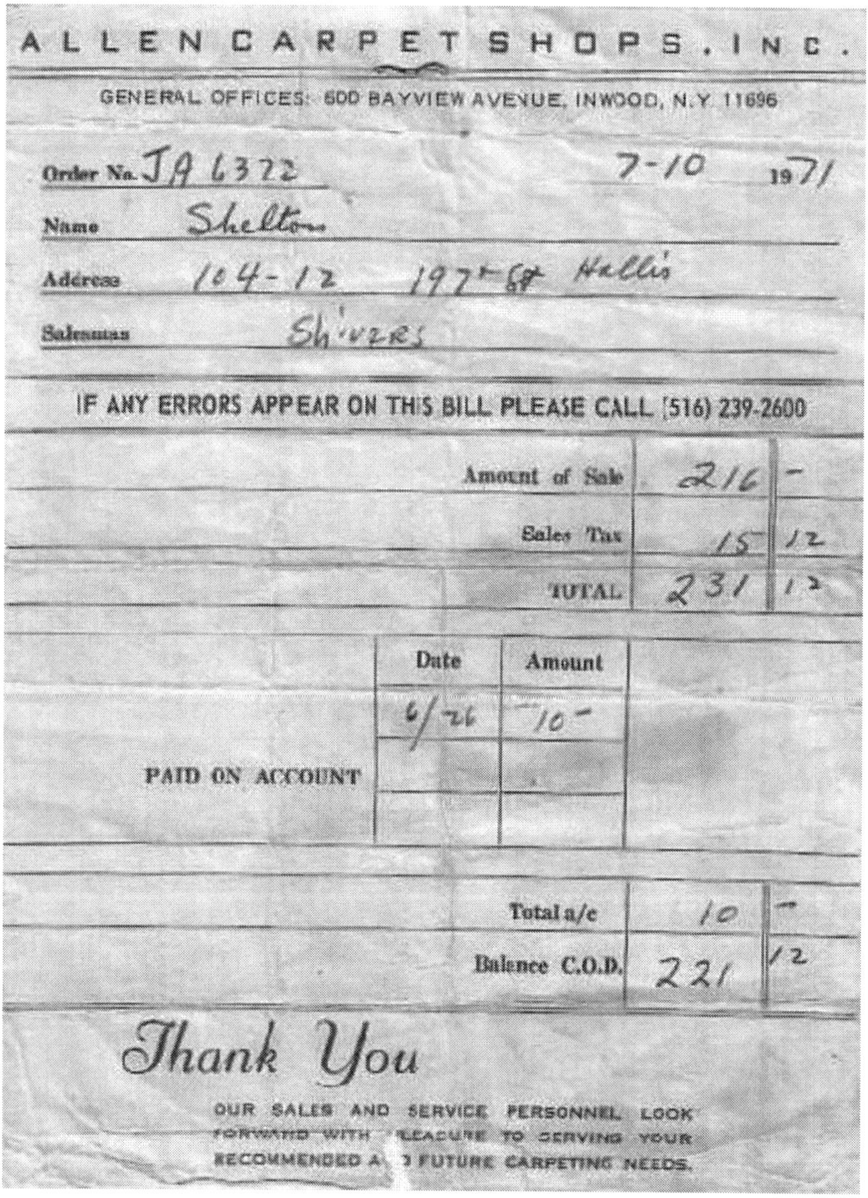

ALLEN CARPET SHOPS, INC.

GENERAL OFFICES: 600 BAYVIEW AVENUE, INWOOD, N.Y. 11696

Order No. JA 6322 7-10 1971

Name Shelton

Address 104-12 197th St Hollis

Salesman Shivers

IF ANY ERRORS APPEAR ON THIS BILL PLEASE CALL (516) 239-2600

Amount of Sale	216	–
Sales Tax	15	12
TOTAL	231	12

PAID ON ACCOUNT

Date	Amount
6/26	10–

Total a/c	10	–
Balance C.O.D.	221	12

Thank You

OUR SALES AND SERVICE PERSONNEL LOOK FORWARD WITH PLEASURE TO SERVING YOUR RECOMMENDED A[illegible] FUTURE CARPETING NEEDS.

Figure 29: Receipt of the first day I met John Shivers, Manager of Allen Carpet

Chapter 40 — My Visit to the Island of Our Father's Birth: The Grand Cayman Island

On July 11, 1971, I was on my way to the Grand Cayman Island, British West Indies, the island of my father's birth. When I was just a child, I had the privilege to meet a number of our father's brothers and one of his uncles during their visits to us in Brooklyn. This was due to their positions as merchant marines that allowed them the opportunity to travel around the world, including the United States of America. Upon their arrival, I was often presented with lots of love, combined with a dollar or two that left me with fond memories of them.

To meet these family members only made me eager to visit the land where they were born and to meet the rest of the paternal side of my family. It would be my first introduction to them, along with my eighteen-month-old son Eric, and for them to become acquainted with us as well.

My father was happy to learn of my interest in meeting his side of the family, and my desire to visit the land of his birth. He chose to drive me and my son to the airport for this was his opportunity to instruct me on where I should go and whom I should meet. As we drove, he described the house where he had lived and the people he'd left behind.

"Estella, make sure you see your Grandfather Swan, Auntie Pom-Pom, and Uncle Dick. Also, try to convince your grandfather that he should come to America and I will cover the expense needed for his ailing eyes."

"Yes, Papa."

"And don't forget to take pictures of the family and especially the house where I lived."

"O.K., Papa. I will."

I was filled with instructions as we approached the airport.

149

Although his instructions were much to remember, they were of interest to me as well. However, my response to his every wish was always, "Yes, Papa."

At the airport, my son and I followed the signs that led us to the proper counter where our luggage was collected. We then headed to the proper gate for departure and in one hour's time we were called to line-up for boarding. While we stood on line, I noticed people scheduled for this flight resembled my ethnicity, for they were mostly all blacks with a handful of whites. It revealed to me what the population of the environment I was visiting would look like.

Hours later after our safe landing, I immediately thanked God for a safe trip. This I remembered to do as we taxied along a much bumpy road toward the area for our exit. As I observed the island through the glass windows, the coconut trees immediately took my attention, for these were identical to those in the place where I was born, Nicaragua. It was as if I was in my native home again.

I wondered why we did not approach an exit building as done in New York. However, I later learned the procedure for exiting an airplane in this country, was to have the steps driven and placed to the exit door of the airplane. We would then walk down these steps to the grounds where we were led into the building.

While standing on line, I noticed my family members waiting to receive us. To see them standing there was quite rewarding and quite comforting. Once I completed the required procedures I took my son's hand and we hurried toward our family. I was greeted with much love and acceptance.

"Hello, Stella. How was your flight?" Uncle Alex inquired with excitement in his voice.

"It was pretty good. Even Eric enjoyed the flight, as he looked through the windows."

"Hello, Stella. I'm so glad you made it," greeted Aunt Ronica.

"Hello Stella," echoed my cousins Al and Nicky.

They were as excited to see me as I was to see them.

"O.K. Let's head to the house," Uncle Alex instructed.

Previous to this travel I requested to stay at the home of my paternal Uncle Alex (Alexander), for I was already familiar with him and his family, since they once resided at our house in America. Now I would meet the rest of the Frederick family, one of the largest land owners in that country.

The next day, I was introduced to as many family members as possible. My grandfather Swan Frederick was the father of fifteen children, my father being his firstborn.

I was prepared to meet an abundance of family members, who turned out to be exactly as my father described them. Including my father, there was a total of six children born from the first wife who died: two girls and four boys. Following her death grandfather married her sister who gave birth to father's additional siblings of two girls and five boys.

Upon my visit, I could only wonder how they all fit into such a small house. In addition to these siblings, my brother was later included.

Figure 30: Grandfather Swan Frederick's House

It was such a pleasure when the children, mostly cousins, went crabbing on my behalf and returned with an abundance of the largest crabs that I had never seen before. My Uncle Alburis went diving, and returned with fresh conchs along with a slew of lobsters only the ocean could hold. Thankfully, my Aunt Ronica was willing to do the cooking, for I would not have known where to begin.

Figure 31: An Island Crab headed to the pot.

Figure 32: Uncle Alburis holding an Island Lobster

Figure 33: Uncle Alburis holding conch meat taken from conch shells like the one below.

Figure 34: Conch in his shell (Dreamstime.com)

There were foods which I could identify, since the Grand Cayman and Nicaragua were similar in their delightful island foods. I became a Nicaraguan all over again, as I peeled the sugar canes stalks with my teeth and picked mangoes and pears (avocados) from the trees that grew all around us.

In addition to such fine cooking, various aunts and cousins baked cakes and delivered them to me. At this time, we were introduced to each other, and they let me know the order of their existence. I was smothered with gifts from various family members and delighted to meet so many cousins, some of whom were close to me in age.

Another delightful experience was that of my visit to Aunt Elsie's house where her husband, Uncle Cleveland, did all the cooking. Our dinner was brought to a table where we sat under a coconut tree on a hill away from the house. There we ate while the tropical winds surrounded us as though it was ordered especially for the occasion. It was as if it blew the words saying, "Thanks for coming."

Uncle Cleveland then picked a number of young coconuts that hung from the trees around us. The juice from the coconut served as our drinks, and its inside were as soft as jelly that served as our dessert. Today, I name that spot from the scene of the movie "**South Pacific.**" Whenever I visit I am sure to stop at that location, for it brings back such fond memories.

Figure 35: Eric at 18 Months

In addition to such acceptance, one day during our stay my son Eric was taken for a horseback ride, although he was only eighteen-months-old. Hopefully, he was forgiven by the horse he rode when he urinated on its back. Unfortunately, the diaper he wore did not hold up to its standards. The expression he made after this spillage was, "I did it," which became a humorous nickname. However, who knew this would be the beginning of his future in horseback riding, for in later years he would become a first-place winner of trophies during his years at camp, at the age of ten.

In addition to this fond visit, I discovered that due to my father being the first born of fifteen children, my siblings and I were gifted with the clout of being "children of the first born". We are all treated with much love and dignity.

During the years of my visits, I continued close ties with the family. I often attended funerals of the many elders, where I would be asked to speak. When our father died at the age of ninety, we were sure to have him buried within the land of his birth. It would be our final gift to him, for this was his desire. He was back home, his final resting place.

Chapter 41 — My Return to the Carpet Store Leads to Marriage

When I returned from vacation, I made certain to visit the carpet store to complete the order by making a final payment, and to arrange a delivery date. John and I talked on various subjects and I made certain to mention that I was dating someone. It was obvious that he was not impressed with the story I told in reference to my then boyfriend, whom I referred to as my "Honey".

Once we completed our small talk, John invited me to dinner. I accepted his invitation and we confirmed the date, time, and place to meet. As I walked toward the bus station, I wondered how silly I must have appeared to the public, while walking with such a silly smile on my face. I left him wondering what this fine gentleman was all about.

On Friday, I received a call to confirm the time for our dinner date and to expect a taxi cab that would drive me to his work place. He then added that it would be my decision to bring my son along for he was also invited. I responded, "Thank you, my son will be in attendance."

It was quite comforting that Eric and I were escorted to our date as though we were dignitaries. We appeared at the carpet store where John waited and soon after we were off to dinner.

During our dinner, John and I, along with little Eric, enjoyed each other's company, as our conversation led us to become more comfortable with each other. When our dinner date ended, I felt it was the beginning of a serious relationship, for we decided to meet again. I will always remember the Italian food — shrimp parmigiana — that I still enjoy after so many years.

On my way to work, I often walked in the same direction in route to the train station, which led me pass the front of John's carpet store. One day I deliberately waved to him then disappeared on the crowded sidewalks, as though I was a ghost in disguise. It was merely a playful game I played.

Later I learned that I was mistaken for his ex-girlfriend Marline. I also discovered the reason John first approached me at his job, was due to the fact that he mistook me for this same person. She and I resembled each other so strongly that people believed we were identical. We were the same height, same complexion, same size, and wore a similar curly wig. One evening while John and I sat in a bar, a stranger who walked in, leaned over to kiss me on the cheeks. However, John stopped him in his tracks only to say "That's not her." I was obviously mistaken for Marline.

That week I called for a private taxi cab. When another cab driver heard through their telephone system of my request and my address, he then called that cab driver, to let him know of his desire to say hello to me in passing. He pulled up to the cab I was in, simply said hello and gave my young son a silver dollar. He believed that I was that other girl, who lived at that (my) address.

I learned later that although we resembled each other so strongly, we were completely different in our behavior. She was heavily involved in the club and bar scene, while I was just the opposite. I was described as "a stay at home type". It bothered me for a while that perhaps my resemblance of this person was the reason John and I came together; however, I won a pot of gold when I landed John.

Soon after, I dismissed the "honey" (Marvin) I was dating, via telephone message. Not being convinced that our short relationship had ended, he immediately appeared at my house for a true understanding. I confirmed to him my previous telephone call that our dating days were over. This breakup was not just because of John, however. It was also due to "honey's" behavior, since he had a habit of accompanying his friends each evening dressed as though they were headed to a good time, and leaving me behind. He had repeated this behavior twice, but there would NOT be a third. He did not play according to my personal rules of play. Unfortunately, he brushed past John on his way out, as John was coming in, for I had invited him to dinner. On entry, John's question to me was, "Is this Grand Central Station?"

I found John to be a perfect gentleman. During our conversation, he revealed to me that he was previously married and planned for divorce. This began our relationship, the one I believed I was looking for. One thing led to another, and following my dismissal of Marvin, John and I became seriously involved. Somehow, he hadn't believed that I was serious about that "honey" I referred to, so he continued in his pursuit that led us into becoming an item.

One evening, I received a telephone call from John. When asked what I was doing, I responded that I was about to watch television; however, I was experiencing difficulty since the TV was not functioning properly. Later that evening I was presented with the delivery of a brand-new television. The delivery was marked "From: John Shivers." It was the greatest impression of him that I or anyone else could have asked for.

Soon after my finding this fine gentleman, two ex-boyfriends revealed their interest in returning to my life, and suddenly, men were falling from the skies. However, I was certain that I had found the one I was looking for.

It became even more baffling when, after five years away, my previous fiancé returned from Trinidad. He was waiting outside of my work place to surprise me and invited to join him for dinner. Again, he was in pursuit of winning my hand in marriage. He confessed that he would leave his wife if I promised to marry him. Unfortunately, I was not interested in his repeated pursuit, for I was simply not in love with him. So, for the second time he returned home without me. This was the final ending of our relationship, for it was my personal rule to always move forward. As the saying goes," When it rains, it pours!"

As time went on, John was always willing to watch little Eric while I shopped. I would return approximately one hour later to find my son enjoying himself while playing with a toy that John had purchased for him. It appeared as though they truly enjoyed each other. This only revealed to me that God had chosen the perfect gentleman for me.

When I completed my errands John often invited me to dinner and Eric was always included. We definitely fit the description of a complete family.

Chapter 42—Our Future Together

Seven months after we began dating, John and I joined hands in matrimony. His legal divorce from his first wife went into effect on February 23, 1972 and the following day we were married. At midnight of our wedding party, John announced that it was now February 25, his birthday. Our marital celebration then changed into a birthday party.

Once we were married, we moved to a high-rise apartment in Queens where we lived on the top floor (the 17th known as the Pent House). There was a balcony leading out from our apartment overlooking the store where John worked and he often waved as he left for work on the weekends.

Living at this apartment was convenient for it was located in the business part of town, making it easy to reach the trains for my travel to and from my place of employment in New York City. It was also helpful when John took on the responsibility to drop off and pickup Eric from school.

A few years later we decided to build a house on a lot given to us by my father, located in Suffolk County, Long Island, the perfect place to raise a family. In September of 1976 our house was ready for occupancy, and along with our son Eric, we moved in.

I often related this community to be a resemblance of my home town in Nicaragua for it gave the appearance of a tropical island. The size of our lot was 100 feet wide and 400 feet long, with an abundance of trees and a small number of houses. There was a golf course with an adjoining lake approximately fifteen minutes walking distance from our house. This neighborhood was so private that it took my written request to the county to have the proper amount of lights awarded to the community. I succeeded with this request and the response was immediate.

Unfortunately, our move to Long Island became a job in itself. It required that I travel a total of four hours a day round trip to reach my place of employment. This travel included one half hour to reach the railroad station in Patchogue; one hour by railroad to New York City, and a half hour between two separate subway trains, in order to reach my final destination. Although I often reported to the office by the required hour of 8.50 a.m., there were often times the trains would arrive later than their scheduled hour of arrival. Luckily, I was never penalized for such lateness; however, I felt it would become an issue in the long run. Therefore, I pondered for a while on whether or not I should retire from the bank I loved so dearly.

On our way to work one morning we knew it was time to retire our positions in the City. As we headed to the Rail Road Station on the Long Island Expressway, we were lucky to escape a deadly accident. The snow and ice build-up caused us to slide from the first lane to the third lane; turned around facing traffic while sliding backward to the first lane.

"Holy smokes, that was close," I said to John, as I shook in fright.

"Yes, it was. Let's just turn around and go home."

"I'll get off at the next exit." After regaining myself, I was finally able to reverse and get the car into the proper direction. We got off the freeway at the next exit. I didn't feel guilty for missing work that day, for we were lucky to have survived. However, I continued this lengthy travel for two years.

Another intelligent decision to leave this area of employment was due to the fact that our house was often broken into and robbed. In the years of residency at this location, we had six robberies and suffered many losses. Our lengthy absence from home allowed too many hours for robbers to break in.

One morning while on our way to work, we noticed young men standing around at a corner where we normally passed on the way to the train station. I felt a sense of danger.

"John, those men look as though they have nothing to do."

"Yes, they appear to be robbers."

"They seem to know that we're on our way to work,"

"Oh well, there's nothing we can do about it, but hope for the best," was John's response.

That evening when we entered our house we smelled smoke and rushed up the stairs assuming there was a fire. Sure enough, there were burnt marks into the wooden floors. The robbers had used lit matches in order to see their way around the house, since dusk had settled in. We concluded that when they heard us come into the house, they ran out through the back doors, which they had already broken.

It was a proven fact that we were away from the house far too many hours.

Chapter 43 — The Birth We Waited For

In the 4th year of our marriage, on December 24, 1976, our baby girl was born. John finally received his Christmas present and we named her Lashonne. We chose this name since its sound is closely to "John". As years went by, her defense when caught with her hands in the cookie jar was to remind us (with a playful smile) that she was our Christmas present!

Baby Lashonne appeared to be identical to her father, and she was certainly God's plan as his Christmas gift. His wish came through for he finally received his baby girl after so many years.

When John and I became husband and wife, Eric gained a father and John gained a son. Following our union together, he always wished for a birth child of his own, hopefully, a girl. Each year whenever I asked what his desire was for a Christmas present his response would be the same, a baby girl.

Four years later when finally becoming pregnant, and after confirmation with my doctor, a thought came to mind of how I should surprise John with this blessed event. Since John surprised me with an engagement ring, it was the reason that gave me the idea of how to present this pregnancy to him. Although I was unable to write a message and placing it into his glass of wine, as he did with my engagement ring, I could place this surprise into the fold of his dinner napkin. I watched him as he unfolded his napkin which contained a picture of an empty baby carriage where I wrote the words "To be filled in nine months."

As John opened his napkin to this message, he looked at me for confirmation.

"Stella, I read this message but do I understand its true meaning?" he asked.

"Yes, indeed ... Surprise. I'm pregnant!"

John sprang from his seat, gave me a hug then silently continued his dinner with a great big smile on his face.

Prior to this pregnancy, it seemed as though I was at the end of my attempt to ever becoming pregnant. It was as though John would never have that daughter he always wished for.

Once John and I accepted the fact that I was never to become pregnant with his baby girl, we finally gave up trying. In order to expand our family, we then registered in the Long Island Foster Care System, for there we began their required classes in order to become eligible to adopt a child. It required that we attend a number of classes in order to fulfill all pre-requisites for qualification.

After our attendance at only a few meetings at the Foster Care System, I received notice from my doctor that I was with child. This report was too good to believe and I needed to find a joyful way to relay this information to John.

This was a blessing that took many days and nights to comprehend, for the years 1973, 74 and 75 went by with my failing to conceive. Although my husband wished for a girl, it did not matter what sex it would be; however, we were delighted to learn that his wish would come true, for I was expecting his baby girl!

Now that Baby Lashonne was born, it was a definite incentive for me to retire. However, I continued this rigorous commute up to the eighth month of my pregnancy. I realized how fortunate I was not to have experience morning sickness, but I often carried a brown paper bag should there be a need for me to vomit. Luckily, I never needed to use that brown paper bag.

To end such lengthy commute was the best decision I could have made, for it also allowed me to care for my seven-year-old son Eric, who was under the care of a baby sitter. John continued his commute indefinitely, with the intention of landing a position nearest to home as well.

Chapter 44—Farewell to My First Place of Employment

After such dangerous travels and the tremendous amount of years I was employed at the bank, I finally made a decision to resign. It was time to end the too-rigorous commute that had continued for two years from Long Island to New York City.

My decision to leave this company, the work place where I reached my adulthood, was extremely difficult; however, the learning experience I gained after serving 14 ½ years, gave me the growth and ability to search for a quality position closer to home.

At the time of departure, I was given a gracious farewell by the many friends whom I considered family. However, I had already accepted the date when I learned that other friends among the employees had also arranged to hold a retirement party on my behalf. Unfortunately, these luncheons were scheduled on the same day and at the same time, which placed me in the position of having to make a choice between the two groups of friends.

My friend Kathy revealed to me her plan to surprise me with an arrangement she had made with our friends.

I was really disappointed. I told her of the other group and that I had accepted their plans. "Kathy, I believe it would be the best decision to meet with them."

"Yes," she responded. "I wasn't aware of their arrangement, since no one ever responded to my inquiry about it, so I went on with my arrangement accordingly. I do understand. It's not your fault, and I'll explain to your other friends what happened."

"I'm so sorry. Please make sure that you explain to them my dilemma. Thanks, Kathy."

I thought it proper to choose my immediate department of

which the Vice President and Treasurer had arranged to take place at their private dining room that included our immediate department only. Because I was unable to join the second group of friends, they went on without me; otherwise, it would have been a loss of their deposit.

The number of gifts I received from these groups of friends was unbelievable. They even remembered to include safety pins, the item used during that era to close cloth diapers. The gifts were so many that it required that I call my husband John for assistance, in order to carry them home.

It was a very sad day to leave this place where I was treated with much love and respect. It was also the company of which I grew into adulthood for I began employment with them at the age of eighteen and now I was thirty-two. My employment at this company was a learning experience that led me to the place I am today. However, for the best interest of my immediate family, I decided to gracefully resign, leaving much love and fond memories behind.

And it was in the best interest of my immediate family, for it was obvious that my absence from our new born infant and my then seven-year-old son would be unfair to them. It was the right decision no matter how sad it was to leave.

By working at the bank, I gained the proper training needed to serve at any future organization. I am forever grateful to them for their friendship and learning experience that I was fortunate to achieve.

Chapter 45—Finding Employment Closer to Home

In 1977, one year after retirement from the bank, it was time that I return to work, for our financial stability was dwindling quite rapidly. I decided to apply for the New York State secretarial examination, and by reaching the required passing grade, I was accepted into the system immediately.

Once I entered into this line of employment, it allowed me the opportunity to accept an offer made by the New York State Department of Transportation, located in Hauppauge, NY. Although it was a lower level position, I accepted their offer as a temporary placement until the more advanced level of which I was qualified would become available, for I was fortunate to receive an offer as a Clerk Typist so quickly.

Although it was at a low-pay salary I considered it to be a prestigious position, since I was given my own private office, and to communicate directly with Albany, NY the Capital. My job was to handle paperwork for all truckers who traveled along the Long Island Expressway, and other designated areas of Long Island. I was responsible to confirm the update of their licenses. Otherwise, I would contact Albany in order that they may fulfill all requirements and to complete their paperwork. I was to ensure their compliance to the rules and regulations of the New York State system, in order that they would receive "acceptance for travel". Another important responsibility was to arrange for police escort to handle all wide-road travels along the Long Island Expressway.

Although this was a temporary position, realizing the short distance of thirty-minutes close to home made it a definite winning argument.

Three months following my employment at this organization I was called to the office of my supervisor.

"Estella, we received information that an offer is being made to you for an interview by Stony Brook University for a higher position," I was informed by my supervisor.

"Oh, yes, I did receive that information just today."

"Well, Stella, we are sorry to lose you to a place that can offer you a higher salary. However, we may be able to elevate your position here with us once a line at your level is available. We hate to lose you."

"Thank you so much, but if I'm offered a higher position, I will accept it. I truly enjoyed my stay with your office, but I need to receive a higher salary."

That day I was contacted for an interview by the Department of Mathematics, at the Stony Brook University. Although I was not certain whether or not I would be accepted for hire, it appeared as though I was on my way to a promising future.

Again, I was leaving an abundance of such fine individuals. Although my presence at this office was cut short, I was fortunate to be amongst some of the finest individuals one could ever ask for. But now I needed to be on my way to a higher standard position.

Chapter 46—Fortunate Employments

To leave my position at the Department of Transportation was another solemn experience. It was sad to leave an office of such friendly individuals but I needed to move forward. When I received a call for an interview at Stony Brook University, Department of Mathematics, I accepted. This interview was for a higher-level position of which I had been tested for and passed. Following my interview, I was offered a secretarial position to begin immediately.

"Thanks for the offer," I said. "However, I need to let you know that I am three months pregnant."

"That's fine, but we believe you are the right choice for this position. You will begin immediately."

At first it was a scary situation for it could have been a cause for rejection. However, I was hired on the spot while filled with joy that my pregnancy was not a deterrent.

I later learned that being upfront with them only added to the reason of my being accepted, for they saw the honesty in me.

On the day of hire I was experiencing abdominal pain. I immediately contacted the doctor's office and while driving there, I held my waistband away from my stomach with one hand, while driving with the other, for I was in tremendous pain. To drive approximately twelve miles in such condition was difficult; however, I needed to reach my doctor's office as soon as possible before something serious should happen.

At the doctor's office, I waited anxiously to hear my name called. The time I waited seemed to last a lifetime, for I was experiencing excruciating pain. Finally, after waiting about half an hour, I responded anxiously to the call of my name.

Upon my entrance to the appointment room, I rushed passed the doctor to the bathroom for I needed to empty my bladder immediately. Unfortunately, it wasn't the urination I believed that was happening, it was a miscarriage. My bladder continued emptying, since the water bag had broken. I couldn't believe I was having a miscarriage.

As I lay on the patient's table, it happened and an ambulance was called. I was immediately rushed to the hospital. The baby was wrapped and laid on my chest. The warmth of that child would remain on my chest for many days afterward.

I knew I wasn't going to be available to begin my new job and my constant fear was that they would hire someone else. However, I had to call the office.

"Hello, Mrs. Cohen. This is Estella. I just want you to know that I am in the hospital. I had a miscarriage."

"Oh, I'm so sorry, Estella. Do take your time in returning to us. Your position will remain open for you."

"Thank you so much for your understanding."

Two weeks later, my recovery complete, I reported to the department to begin my new job … the same position I'd been hired for.

My employment at this department was a pleasurable experience. I worked hard, and as accurate as possible, which allowed me the opportunity for advancement to a higher position, as private secretary to the Chairman of the Department of Mathematics. Some wondered how I managed so well with this chairman, for he was known as a person of "strictly business and very stern". Well, so was I.

Later I received compliments on my handling of overseas calls. This was an area that I was most familiar with, for I was previously employed at a foreign bank where this was a requirement. It was brought to my attention that the previous employee, who handled such telephone calls, was said to have sounded like a truck driver. Therefore, I was most welcomed for placing such calls.

I became popular for my typing skills, and was often selected by many professors and graduate students to type their books, papers, and theses. Since the awareness of my willingness to accept after hours typing, I received extra work from various individuals to conduct additional typing jobs at home.

One most remembered deadline was that of a professor who stood at my house while I typed. This was a twenty-four-hour typing responsibility. He had to meet his submission deadline for an article. I typed, he proof-read, and so it went....

We met the deadline. I expressed to this gentleman that the deadline we attempted to meet, was definitely a reminder of the time my previous workplace caught on fire. There I was told that the boss would throw water on me while I typed, in order to meet a deadline. It was time for laughter by working so hard.

By working at this capacity, it allowed me and my husband the additional financial ability to send our three children to private schools (Catholic Schools) and colleges. I worked in the day, and later at home during the night. I am honored to have been acknowledged in these writings and today, there are many holding my name of acknowledgement, stored on the shelves at this department.

On several occasions, I would hear my husband as he called out, "Stella, when are you coming to bed?"

"I'm coming," was always my response, in hopes that he would fall back to sleep.

My typing at night was a race between me and the harmony of birds, as well as the cackling of chickens in the neighborhood. I tried racing them to bed before they began their chattering that started at 5:00 a.m. each morning. However, these creatures won every time, since I only got to bed at 6:00 a.m. They began their chatter before my head would hit the pillow. Due to the fact that I was expected at work by 8:30 a.m., I never had much sleep.

Later, I continued upgrading my position by taking the required New York State examinations. By passing such exams, I had the opportunity for hire by the Stony Brook University Medical Center, as Administrative Assistant to the Deputy Director of Nursing, for whom I worked seven years—until she retired. Her retirement was the cause for me to submit my application for the position as Administrative Assistant to the Director of Radiology where I was accepted.

Seven years later I decided to look into a more interesting position. After giving a courteous notice to my supervisor stating my intention to leave, I accepted two interviews. Following these interviews, I was immediately offered a position by two separate departments. I thereby accepted the position as Administrative Assistant to the Director of Media Relations.

While working in the Media Relations Department, I had the opportunity to operate as "TV camera woman" for Channel 27— Health Relation Station that partnered with the hospital to discuss medical issues, and where specialty medical doctors along with their patients were interviewed. These specialty issues regarded new developments and findings, etc., coordinated by hospital personnel and hospital leaders.

Another important responsibility was to organize press conferences to include radio, newspaper, and television personnel. The purpose for these press conferences was to avoid the disruption of patients by having them scheduled for individual interviews. Other coverage consisted of various medical/hospital personnel on important medical issues for the benefit of the public.

I was honored when offered the responsibility to arrange the re-enactment of an incident, to be covered by a Japanese Movie Production Company. This company traveled around the world filming interesting medical stories. The re-enactment was that of an individual who lost his two hands—cut off just below the wrist—at his place of work, and reattached by a team of doctors at Stony Brook University Hospital. After a year's time and by attending physical training, the patient returned to driving his car and became self-reliant.

One most remembered responsibility was to supervise over sixty police officers. This was due to my availability when staying after hours to catch up on daily responsibilities. Unfortunately, the head supervisors of my department were not in reach for it was much too late after their work schedule, and the need was immediate.

That night I was called to a patient floor by a hospital administrator for immediate assistance. There was a need to handle a crowd of police officers and to have them removed from the floor. These officers were visiting one of their fallen men. Unfortunately, they produced an abundance of noise and made the patients nervous.

In ten minutes' time, I was successful in having a comfortable and private area made ready to place these officers and directed them from the floor. My task was then to transport six individuals at a time (to and from) to visit their fallen officer. I had to make several trips up and down the elevators until all visitors were fully satisfied. This responsibility was successfully achieved and all went well. An E-mail of acknowledgement was sent by their head officer thanking our office for our graciousness. Our department was highly praised.

Finally, I was also responsible for issuing press releases to various media organizations, and to the public, where they were invited to receive specialty environmental issues, to bring awareness to the public.

Chapter 47—Our Second Birth

In 1980, I gave birth to our second baby girl and we named her Kai-Yvonne. The race to John's lap between his baby girls had begun, and he received them with open arms. Now that he had his two girls, this would be my final successful delivery of birth.

Our son Eric became a big brother to his two baby sisters and he was delighted with this position that he handled so well. With so many years between Eric and his little sisters, life between them was never a challenge, and they show extreme love for their big brother as well!

I was fortunate that during each of my pregnancies, I was awarded with gifts from my colleagues at work. I received all that was needed for a new birth and I am forever thankful and grateful to all those who made my life much easier by their kindness.

Two years later, I was fortunate to become pregnant with a baby boy. Unfortunately, my attempt to bare this baby failed, for the miscarriage took place within the seventh month of my pregnancy. That night I drove to the hospital for I was in excruciating pain. Soon after my arrival, I miscarried. It happened just a few hours prior to my next doctor's appointment. Unfortunately, working too many late nights resulted in this miscarriage. This would be the last. I made my decision to never become pregnant again.

I can only thank God for the gift of pregnancies I was allowed to have.

Chapter 48—The Visit to Alice's Home

In 1969, about 35 years after our separation from Alice (our stepmother's niece), my sister Glenda and I bravely visited her for she was suffering from a deadly illness. Surprisingly enough we were allowed entry.

While visiting this family, we became involved in a roundtable discussion, for the children and their mother were always accepted at my house, which they visited on several occasions. We shared fond memories with them of the time we first met their mother; when she was only ten. They listened attentively and it was as if we gained a newfound family.

The purpose for this visit was to console Alice's children. Thankfully, the children showed complete acceptance toward us for they knew their mother had no hard feelings against us, that was solely the behavior of their grandmother Serena.

Unfortunately, not much later Alice's illness overcame her and she left this earth at the age of sixty-five. She left an abundance of five children and many grandchildren.

Later, my sister and I decided that in order to keep peace, we would remain away from their place of residency.

It is my sincere belief that Alice was not responsible for the ugly treatment toward us during our childhood days, for it became obvious to me that she was definitely influenced by her mother. Thank God, we made peace with each other before she died.

May Alice rest in peace!

Chapter 49—Dedication to Our Father

On January 24, 1998 our father, Lyn Hurst Frederick, left this earth to a better place. It is my strong belief that he is in Heaven. My sister Glenda and I took his ashes to his home on the Grand Cayman Island for burial, and to be with his other deceased and beloved family members.

Our father's love, care, compassion, and understanding, will remain in my heart forever!

It is obvious to me that he always had us, his children, in his thoughts and mind. He was determined to carry out his parental responsibility, as he promised us to do. This he definitely achieved when bringing us from Nicaragua to America, to provide the proper care as a devoted parent.

Papa taught us to stay on the right path, remain good citizens, and to follow in his footsteps. He expected us to provide the proper care for our offspring; for he believed it is our responsibility.

I can truly say that we, his children, have kept to his standards! I am also sure that he left this earth knowing and witnessing for himself that we have lived up to his training, for we surely owe that to him. It would have been a sin to let him down!

May you rest in peace, Papa. I love you so, so much!!

Papa's Farewell - He left this Earth a few days after taking this photo.

Figure 36: The Frederick Family – (L to R) – Eleanor, Estella, Orlando, Glenda. Seated in front: Papa Lyn Hurst Frederick.

Chapter 50—High School Reunion

On August 23, 2002, I attended my high school reunion at Prospect Heights High School in Brooklyn. There I found the school to be in the same condition as it was the day I graduated in 1962. Its brass doorknobs were still shining, its indoor steps were the same white marble stones, and the pool was still in perfect condition. It was obvious that the school's principals throughout the years had kept up with the pride of this school. Its current principal made certain that each graduate's next step was to attend college. Their GPAs were in the upper 70s and 90s, and the students were quite impressive!

When touring the school, I found the lockers to be in bright colors. Each group of lockers had their own color, separate from those on other floors. They were yellow, red, and green. The class rooms appeared to look the same, and impressively clean. The desks were in the best condition as they were the day I left.

Although the doors to the pool were locked, I was successful in taking a photo through the glass area of its doors. While standing there, taking in the aroma of the pool, it brought back old memories, especially the day I went under waters and was rescued by the swimming teacher. The long stick she stretched out for us to hang on to if we were in trouble truly saved my life as she pulled me to safety.

It was required that we swim from the deep to the shallow end of the pool and return to the deep end. If we achieved this, we would receive a passing grade. It was mandatory to pass the swimming test in order to graduate. I was privileged to receive these swimming lessons for most schools did not offer such training.

To become a stronger swimmer, I decided to join the afterschool swimming program known as the "Dip Club."

However, one day after swimming lesson, I discovered that the distant walk home in the cold winter's snow, with wet hair and sneakers was too much to bear. I was so uncomfortable, I quit.

Upon my return for my graduation class reunion, I found it interesting to see how the ethnicity of the school had changed. It now consisted of mostly black students and a very few whites. This group of students would be the last graduating class under its original school's name. This school would soon turn into a four-small-high-school situation, known as: The Brooklyn School for Music and Theater; The International High School at Prospect Heights; and The Brooklyn Academy for Science.

We elders were given the honor of leading the last graduating class of Prospect Heights H.S. into the auditorium, and the speaker was a motivational speaker who was represented by a movie entitled "Coach Carter".

Prospect Heights High School was a great school from the days I attended and it was impressive to see how well it lasted. This graduating class made me proud to be a graduate of Prospect Heights High School, Class of 1962."

"ALL HAIL TO PROSPECT HEIGHTS HIGH SCHOOL!!"

Chapter 51—The Frederick Family Reunion & John's Visit to Grand Cayman Island

In later years, I was successful by my encouragement to conduct a family reunion. As a result, the **"Frederick Family Reunion, Grand Cayman Island, July 18, 2003"** was begun and became the description affixed to our T-shirts. I was successful in supplying over 200 T-shirts representing this reunion. These shirts were distributed to family members of all sizes while they attended this affair. There was enough food, drinks and much laughter that will always be remembered. By having such a large number of family members, I knew it would be necessary for me to return, in order to meet them all, and our family reunion has made it possible.

On March 2, 2007, my husband John finally joined me on a trip to this great island that I had often told him about. Upon our arrival, he immediately became curious by the sight of the famous Donald Trump's airline that was parked next to our landing space. This would be the beginning of his curiosity.

Shortly after our arrival my family members immediately prepared a large dinner in our honor. Suddenly there were a multitude of foods that encountered a variation of Cayman Island foods. The amount of foods along with the amount of family members seemed as though someone snapped their fingers and it was the makings of a miracle of food and a multitude of family members gathered at once. This togetherness was at the place of a cousin's house located towards a lake overlooking an abundance of boats as they passed by. A multitude of family members were everywhere.

Unbeknown to John, when he said he wasn't ready to eat, no one else would place food on their plates. However, I explained to him that he was the guest of honor, and no one would eat before he did. He immediately understood the situation and filled his plate, giving others the O.K. for them to proceed. This was not an honor he expected to receive, nor was he familiar with.

John immediately became overwhelmed by such acceptance when visiting this great land, especially when treated with such love and dignity he received from people he had never met before.

Becoming acquainted with my Frederick family is an honor for it is the place of my father's birth. By him, we are truly connected and this is proven by the love and respect I, along with my immediate family receives, for they showed extreme love toward us. My sister Glenda has also visited along with her son Clifford. Glenda has become a part of our inclusion in these visits and has truly reflected her feelings to be the same.

Today I continue visiting this beautiful island, for there are so many loved ones living there, while the spirit of my father lingers amongst us. When I do visit, there are many loving family members whom I will always hold close to my heart! For this is the "FREDERICK FAMILY". Yes, that is my maiden name that I am proud to be a part of!

I feel that the blood of the Cayman Islanders and Nicaraguans are intertwined through us. Although these islands are a distance apart from each other; they are similar in many ways. Their foods, fruit and warmth, along with many other attributes, always makes me feel at home. The exception to these similarities is the accents and languages (with Nicaragua being a Spanish speaking country); however, we truly understand each other.

Chapter 52—Retirement

During 2007, several business companies began to fall. The economy of the country collapsed, and most countries around the world were facing financial difficulty. Since John's place of employment folded, we began to experience financial difficulty that lasted six months. However, a few months later John was fortunate to receive employment at another carpet company. Unfortunately, in just a few months later that company also folded. He then applied to a third company where he continued employment for approximately one year, while he successfully waited for me to retire.

In April 2007, I reached a decision that it was time to join my husband in "holy retirement." After my completion of 14 ½ years with J. Henry Schroder Banking Corporation, and 30 years under the auspices of the New York State System, I decided that 44 ½ years of employment was enough. Also, the juggling of work hours between our children and their calendar of events was difficult but finally over. It was as if I was struck by lightning to reach this decision, so I approached my husband for his opinion.

"John, I've decided to retire."

"Well, I'm glad to hear that. Now we can make future plans on where we will spend our last years together."

Soon after, I submitted my notice of retirement.

On the last day of employment, I was gracefully honored with a farewell party. This party was truly overwhelming, for over one-hundred attendees, as well as the CEO of this great organization, were in attendance. There was enough food and dessert for everyone and the gifts I received were five $100 gift checks; one watch; a book entitled *Stella Luna*; a video of my communicating with various employees; and one 2x3 foot photo montage of various news reported occasions that I had been responsible in supervising. These gifts were in remembrance of the work I had done, and the love shown to me by my colleagues.

Please join us as we say farewell to
Estella Shivers

Figure 37: Estella V. Frederick Shivers at her retirement party

During this gathering, a film of my involvement with various individuals was continually playing in the room where we gathered. Finally, I presented my goodbye speech and wished everyone a fond farewell.

Chapter 53—Our Move to a Retirement Community

Soon after my retirement, the paternal grandparents of our grandson gave my husband and me their opinion on a retirement community known as The Villages, located in Florida. They had recently gained residency there. We went, we saw, we conquered.

Six months later my husband and I relocated to this beautiful community. It is also beneficial to our grandson, for it is to his advantage to visit his two sets of grandparents at the same time. His one airline ticket would serve these two purposes. There are often times we grandparents dine out together, which makes little Devonté the center of attention.

Retirement was the best decision I could have made. My husband John and I have chosen to live in this place that is considered to be the fastest growing retirement community in America. Its members are extremely friendly, there's always much to do, and it is known to be heaven for golfers.

John is highly involved in billiards. My involvement includes water aerobics, creative writing, volunteering at a community hospital, and line dancing at the Squares along with a multitude of lovely new friends. I recently joined a Methodist church where I'm involved with a group in making pillows and beautiful pillow cases designed for children of all ages. These pillows are distributed to various organizations that are especially involved in serving young underprivileged children.

My husband and I have decided to remain with this congregation, for it is our belief that God's presence is within those gathering in His name. As a child in Nicaragua, I was baptized Anglican, and once coming to America, I was baptized Catholic. As a child, my husband was baptized Baptist where he was extremely an active member.

We continue the enjoyment of retirement while living in this beautiful place. As we sit on our lanai and look beyond our white picket fence and green grass, it only confirms to me what I was told as a child: "If you work hard you will earn all that life has to offer."

Retirement is great and we are blessed to live in the best country in the world, the United States of America. It was indeed a long journey to the white picket fence and green grass, but here I am ... I made it! May God Bless the United States of America! Amen, Amen, Amen!

Author's Notes

1. My way of contributing to society started at the age of 15. This effort began by my offering assistance at a Catholic Church in Brooklyn, NY. There we provided religious summer classes for underprivileged children in preparation of their effort to receive Holy Communion and Confirmation. We provided games, free lunch, movies (at a made-up theatre in their gym area), assisted with trips to Coney Island Amusement Park and beach. During the winter storms, I assisted with the distribution of food to the elders at their home.

2. Later during my adult years, I joined membership with the Helping Hand Friendly Club of Gordon Heights of Coram, New York. Along with 12 to 15 other elderly citizens, we offered scholarship awards to children in this underserved community. There we became the highest financial contributors of this kind, offering $10,000+ annually. These awards are presented at their High School Award Night. A special luncheon is also held in their honor, along with their parents at a standing hotel.

3. When moved to Florida I became a volunteer at a community hospital, reaching 560+ hours, the goal I set for myself. My jobs were to clean two coffee rooms, brew coffee for patients' visitors, serve ice water to each and every patient at their bedside, and to wheel discharged patients to their loved ones at their car located at the patient pick-up area.

    During my distribution of patients' needs, I offer jokes causing them laughter that serves as a moment of relief from their ailment; I often sat with those waiting for a conversation.

The ice water I serve is distributed with a smile while letting them know that it's "God's Champagne." This serves as a way to assist in lightening their ailments, if even for a moment. They received this offer with a smile.

4. I assist at a church in making pillows and pillow-cases designed especially for children. These pillows are distributed at homes for underprivileged children.

Will I ever retire? Who knows?

****

I have only one more anecdote to share …

Years ago, John would tell people that not only did he meet his future wife, me, while a manager at Allen Carpets; he also met a future president.

On a cold winter day in 1972 this future president came into the carpet store and asked if he could wait there for his ride. John gave him permission to wait in the warmth of the store.

Forty-five years later, on January 20, 2017, Donald Trump was inaugurated as the **45**th **president** of the United States. Perhaps President Trump may remember that day; I'm certain I would remember if someone offered me escape from the cold.

Congratulations President Donald Trump, may your days be as successful as I hope ours will be under your presidency.

###

Figure 38: The Shivers Family

(L to R) John C. and Kai-Yvonne with baby Jon'elle, Estella & John S., Lashonne, Devonté, Joel, Jadalyn, Terrell & Eric, Brianna with baby Lamar. Seated in front: babies JaLia & Eryka.

Made in the USA
Columbia, SC
21 November 2018